The Institute of Biology's
Studies in Biology no. 22

Animal Skeletons

by John D. Currey D.Phil.
**Professor of Biology,
University of York**

Edward Arnold

© John D. Currey, 1970

First Published 1970
by Edward Arnold (Publishers) Limited,
25 Hill Street,
London, W1X 8LL

Reprinted 1972
Reprinted 1975

Boards ISBN: 0 7131 2283 8
Paper   ISBN: 0 7131 2284 6

Printed in Great Britain by
The Camelot Press Ltd, Southampton

General Preface to the Series

It is no longer possible for one textbook to cover the whole field of Biology and to remain sufficiently up to date. At the same time students at school, and indeed those in their first year at universities, must be contemporary in their biological outlook and know where the most important developments are taking place.

The Biological Education Committee, set up jointly by the Royal Society and the Institute of Biology, is sponsoring, therefore, the production of a series of booklets dealing with limited biological topics in which recent progress has been most rapid and important.

A feature of the series is that the booklets indicate as clearly as possible the methods that have been employed in elucidating the problems with which they deal. Wherever appropriate there are suggestions for practical work for the student. To ensure that each booklet is kept up to date, comments and questions about the contents may be sent to the author or the Institute.

1970

INSTITUTE OF BIOLOGY
41 Queen's Gate
London, S.W.7

Preface

In the past thirty years or so the study of skeletons has been to a very large extent the study of their growth and of their physiological relations with the rest of the body. Often the mechanical aspects of their function have been taken for granted. Recently, however, probably because of advances that have been made in the understanding of the properties of man-made materials, and because of the increasing co-operation between engineers and orthopaedic surgeons, there has been an increase in the study of skeletons considered as mechanical systems. This book treats animal skeletons from this point of view.

Most people consider skeletons to be rigid structures, but I have included a chapter on hydrostatic skeletons because they perform many of the functions of more conventional skeletons.

The first chapter may in places seem like a text book on mechanics. Unfortunately skeletons are mechanical things and an introduction to mechanical principles is necessary. However, after the first chapter things become smoother.

Cleveland, Ohio. 1970   J.D.C.

Contents

The Form and Function of Skeletons   1

Apart from maintaining the static shape of an animal, skeletons have two main functions, to act as levers, so that muscles can do useful work, and to act as a protection. In this chapter we shall look at skeletons first as levers then as a protection. When thinking about structures such as skeletons that have forces acting on them it is possible to consider them as quite rigid and strong, or else as deformable, and capable of being broken. We shall first consider them as completely rigid and strong.

1.1 The rigid skeleton

For want of a better word I shall use the word 'element' frequently in this book. It means a single part of a skeleton, such as a single bone or a stiff part of an arthropod limb, between two joints. Skeletal elements act on the environment because they are forced to do so by muscles. The force exerted by the muscles will tend to move the element round a pivot, usually a joint, so that the element exerts a force somewhere else. The ratio of the force exerted by the element and the force exerted by the muscle is the mechanical advantage of the muscle. Sometimes it is important that the element exerts a large force, sometimes that it moves quickly. This is shown in Fig. 1–1, comparing the forelimb of the horse (Fig. 1–1(a)) and the

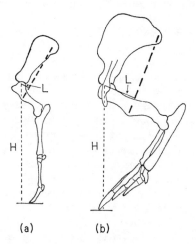

(a)   (b)

Fig. 1–1   The forelimb of the horse (a) and the armadillo (b). The scales have been altered to make the limbs of roughly the same size.

armadillo (Fig. 1–1(b)). The horse needs to move its legs very quickly, but the force they exert need not be very great. Therefore the moment arm of the teres major (L), the muscle swinging the humerus back round the pivot of the shoulder joint, is small compared with the moment of the toe about the shoulder joint (H). In fact L/H is 1/13. This means that the teres major has to exert a force thirteen times greater than that exerted by the toe in the horizontal direction. On the other hand the toe moves thirteen times faster than the insertion of the teres major into the humerus. In comparison the armadillo needs a powerful digging stroke but speed is relatively unimportant. L/H is 1/5·1. The velocity magnification is much less but the force of the toe, compared with the force of the muscle, is correspondingly greater than in the horse. This shows how the same basic apparatus becomes modified in different animals for different purposes. A similar comparison can be made in the case of the myriapod arthropods. The millipedes (diplopods) burrow through the earth, and their legs are stubby and hardly reach beyond the sides of the body. This enables the millipedes to exert a slow but large force. On the other hand the centipedes (chilopods) are active carnivores, running down their prey, and speed is important. They have long slender legs and the muscles moving them have a considerable mechanical disadvantage, but a considerable velocity advantage.

The evolution of the ceratopsian dinosaurs showed a similar state of affairs, but here the differences are in the same group at different geological times. The ceratopsians had scissor-like teeth for chopping tough vegetation, and the *force* of the bite was of the greatest importance. In early ceratopsians the moment arm of the main jaw muscles about the jaw articulation was $\frac{1}{2}$ the moment arm of the middle of the tooth row about this articulation. However, twenty-five million years later the descendants of the early dinosaurs had jaws in which the mechanical advantage of the muscles was changed greatly, being 1/1·05. Natural selection had brought this about by increasing the distance between the articulation and the insertion of the muscles, and decreasing the distance between the tooth row and the articulation by moving the teeth back along the jaw.

The arrangement of the skeletal elements must be considered in relation to the muscles that are going to act on them. In a typical mammalian skeleton, such as that of the mouse, the legs support the weight of the body and when seen from the front are almost vertical. However, seen from the side they are considerably angled, and this means that muscles must be acting around all the joints to keep the legs from folding up. In general each joint has at least one pair of antagonistic muscles acting around it. This implies that when one muscle of such a pair contracts the other will be extended by the resulting movement. Often the muscles are of very different sizes, according to the forces that must be exerted. Jaw-closing muscles are much more powerful than jaw-opening ones, and usually muscles that straighten limbs are more powerful than those that flex them, because it is when being straightened that the skeleton is pushing against the ground. In tetrapods the spinal column supports the weight of the body, and so will tend to sag in the middle. This sagging is prevented by the muscles below the spine which are attached to it and which contract and so tend to push the ends of the spine, which is bowed upwards, together. The muscles tend therefore to compress the spine and are themselves in a state of tension. This is the fundamental state of affairs in skeletons—the stiff elements are loaded in compression, often bending moments acting as well, while the muscles and tendons are loaded in tension. Because they are not stiff they cannot support any bending moments at all. In this way each part of the muscular and skeletal system is exposed to forces it is best able to bear.

1.2 The deformable skeleton

We must start with a few definitions. If a tensile or compressive force is applied to an object of length L it will change in length by an amount ΔL. The ratio $\Delta L/L$ is called the *strain*. If an object is twisted, so that lines at right angles cease to be at right angles, the difference between the new angle and a right angle, measured in radians, is called the *shear strain*. When forces act on a body, *stresses* are set up within it. The forces are, as it were, transmitted through the body by the cohesion of the atoms within it. If we take any small plane in the body we can say that the stresses on the plane are the forces that that small plane exerts on the plane next to it, divided by the area of the plane. Stress is measured in terms of force per unit area, and can be imagined as the intensity of the forces acting on any particular part of a body. (The unit area is the area *after* the force has acted. This is effectively the same as the original area for stiff materials like bone, but for rubber-like substances the area may change considerably on loading.) When the atoms of the material are coming closer together the material is undergoing compressive strain, when they are moving further apart, tensile strain, and when they are moving past each other, shear strain. The last may be difficult to visualise. For instance, suppose a short column is loaded in compression by a weight on its top end. Atoms will be pushed closer to their neighbours in the direction of the length of the column, and so will be undergoing compressive strain. But atoms will also, to some extent, be moved *past* those neighbours that do not lie in the direction of the length of the column. This can be seen by drawing two squares on an india rubber, one with sides in the direction of and at right angles to the long axis of the rubber, and the other with its sides at 45° to the long axis. If you push the ends of the rubber together, the dimensions of the sides in the first square will be altered, but not the angles, while in the second square the angles will be altered. Drawing patterns on rubber and squashing the rubber about is a useful way to gain insight into the relationships between forces and strains.

If an element is loaded in some way we can plot the strain associated with the various stresses. The resulting curve is called a stress-strain curve. A typical one is shown on the left of Fig. 1–2. Consider the curve OABC. In the region OA the strain is directly proportional to the stress. In this

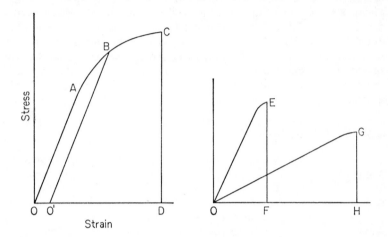

Fig. 1–2   Some diagrammatic stress/strain curves.

region, if the stress is removed, the strain will return to zero. If the strain can return to zero the material of the element is said to be behaving elastic-ally, and the strain is *elastic* strain. Beyond the point A, however, the curve bends over. If the load is removed when the material has reached the point B it will not lose all its strain, but will remain deformed to the extent O-O′. This permanent strain is called *plastic* strain. The stress at which the mater-ial ceases to be elastic and starts to show some plastic strain is called the *elastic limit*. In this case it is the stress at A. With increasing strain the curve gets flatter and flatter until the material breaks at C. The value of CD is the ultimate stress of the material, and for the purposes of this book it is what we shall consider as the strength of the material. (In engineering practice the elastic limit is usually of more interest than the ultimate stress. I shall not use it because its value is known for hardly any biological skeletal material, and because most skeletal materials do not show a great deal of plastic flow and so, unlike say steel, their ultimate stress is not much greater than their elastic limit.) The area under the stress-strain curve, up to any particular stress, is a measure of the amount of work per unit volume that has to be performed on the material in order to achieve that stress. If we take the breaking stress then the area is, in effect, a measure of the amount of energy that can be absorbed before the material fails. The greatest amount of energy is not necessarily absorbed by the material with the highest ultimate stress. This is shown by a comparison of the curves

OEF and OGH. EF is greater than GH, but the latter curve has a greater area under it. Energy absorption is important when an element is loaded very quickly, by impact.

One further point. The less the strain for a given stress, the stiffer the material. In the elastic region engineers talk about the *modulus of elasticity*. This is the value of the stress divided by the strain, the values being taken in that part of the curve where the material is still elastic. (From now on I shall refer to the modulus of elasticity as 'E'.) Most stiff materials start to become plastic, having reached their elastic limit, at strains of less than 0·005. Most fibrous materials do not have stress-strain curves like Fig. 1–2, and E depends on how much they have been stretched. However, this is a somewhat complex point which we shall pursue a little further in Chapter 3. Now we have considered the basic facts of the strength of materials, we must look at the way skeletons are loaded in life.

If a uniform straight element is being loaded in the direction of its long axis, then the stress in any part is given by P/A, where P is the load and A is the cross-sectional area. Such a simple loading system is not often found except in the case of tendons and muscles, which are loaded in tension in this way. The centra of vertebrae are probably loaded in almost pure compression, and the legs of an elephant standing still may act as simple pillars. But the great graviportal legs of elephants are exceptional, and animals that move around at all rapidly cannot have massive skeletons, and those of all moving animals are usually loaded in extremely complex ways that are very difficult to analyse. However, by keeping to a rather simple approach, we can make out some general principles.

The demands of lightness, and strength or stiffness compete with each other, and the skeletons of today are the results of natural selection acting over the years to produce the best compromise between these features. If the skeleton of, say, a gibbon were made more massive and therefore stronger it would be less likely to break when the gibbon made a clumsy landing. However, because the skeleton would be heavier, the gibbon would be less agile, would be more likely to make clumsy landings, and would have to expend more energy hauling its skeleton about the trees. In fact a study showed that over a third of the gibbons shot in the wild had healed fractures of bones, showing the compromise to be a finely balanced one.

1.3   Exoskeletons and endoskeletons

The most obvious difference among the skeletons of mobile animals is that between endoskeletons and exoskeletons. Vertebrates have endoskeletons, and most of the soft tissues of the body are outside the skeleton. Arthropods have exoskeletons, and the skeleton is on the outside. It is always said that mechanically the exoskeleton is more efficient, and we must see why.

When the limb of an animal breaks it is nearly always because it has been bent or twisted too much. Bending loads are particularly dangerous as much lower forces are required to produce large stresses in bending than in axial loading. Imagine a beam, supported at each end, loaded with a weight in the middle. What will be the stresses in the beam? The stress will be different in different places. The beam will sag, the upper surface will become concave, and will be shorter than the lower, convex surface. (Try bending an india rubber to see this.) As, within limits, stress is proportional to strain, the upper part of the beam will be compressed, and the lower part stretched. Half way through, the beam will be neither compressed nor stretched, and apart from small and unimportant shearing stresses, will not be stressed at all. This stress-free part is called the neutral plane and, at any particular section of the beam, the stress in any small part of the section will be directly proportional to its distance from the neutral plane. The bending produced by the load in the middle will be greatest underneath the load and will diminish to zero at each end. So the places with the greatest stress are going to be the top and bottom surfaces of the beam in the middle of the beam. If the beam is going to break it will break first where the stress is greatest; so we are not interested in any average stress, but in the greatest stress. The value of the greatest stress is given by $\sigma_{max} = MR/I$, where σ_{max} is the greatest stress, M is the bending moment at the particular place being considered, R is the greatest distance from the neutral plane there, and I is the second moment of area. The second moment of area is given by $I = \sum y^2 \, \delta A$ where δA is the area of a very small part of the section a distance y from the neutral plane. Going back to the previous equation we see that if the maximum stress is to be low I must be high. As I is made up of areas of bits of the section times the *square* of their distance from the neutral plane it is obviously advantageous, for a given area and therefore weight, to have as much as possible of the material as far as possible from the neutral plane. Material near the neutral plane is not, as it were, pulling its weight. The I-shaped steel beams used in making steel-framed buildings employ this principle. The flanges at the top and bottom resist the bending, the function of the web is to resist shearing stresses and to keep the two flanges apart. In life, skeletal elements are likely, in the extreme and dangerous situation like a fall, to be loaded from any direction, and so the flange is built all the way round and the web is dispensed with. The result is a hollow, tubular skeletal element. Furthermore, twisting or torsional loading can often be dangerous, and for this kind of loading a hollow cylindrical shape is extremely efficient. For these reasons, even endoskeletons have hollow elements, though this may be difficult to make out in such flattened elements as the scapula.

Considering bending again, for a hollow cylinder I is given by $I = (\pi/4)(R^4 - r^4)$, where R and r are the external and internal radii respectively (Fig. 1–3). If the cross-sectional area of the cylinder is a constant, say A, we can find out how the value of I alters as R alters. (Obviously, as the external radius is increased the cylinder must become thinner-walled to keep A constant.) It turns out that $I=(A/2)(R^2-(A/2\pi))$. Another thing we can consider is the rigidity. The less an element deflects for a given load, the more rigid it is said to be. This is often more important than strength. Deflection is proportional to $1/I$, so the rigidity of the element is proportional to I. Now, in the particular case of a cylinder the R's in the two formulae are the same, so the maximum stress is proportional to R/I, and the lower its value the greater the force needed to break the element. Therefore I/R is equivalent to strength in bending. We can make a table giving values for R, I and I/R. We assume that the area is a constant and is such, with the elimination of some constants, as to make the value of I equal to 1 when R equals 1.

External radius R	1	2	4	10
I (proportional to rigidity)	1	7	31	199
I/R (proportional to strength)	1	3·5	7·8	19·9

The rigidity goes up very rapidly as R increases, and the strength also increases, though less rapidly (Fig. 1–3). Therefore, if an animal can afford only a certain weight of skeleton it would be advantageous, for resisting bending, to have the skeleton outside the soft tissues. Similar arguments apply to torsional loading. It would seem that mechanically the arthropods have an advantage over the vertebrates in their skeletal arrangements. But all optimal situations in this world are a compromise, so we must look for disadvantages stemming from the possession of an exoskeleton. And there

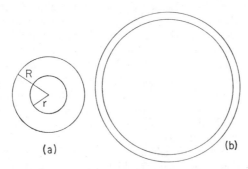

Fig. 1–3   The annulus in (b) has the same area as (a), but it has a value for I that is 5·8 times as great, and a value for I/R 2·9 times as great.

are some. First, as the value of R gets larger, for a constant cross-sectional area the walls must get thinner, and eventually they will get so thin that the skeleton will collapse. The material will not have broken, but will have buckled. A tin can will collapse in this way if loaded in compression, torsion or bending. This buckling, called local buckling, depends on the stiffness, not on the strength of the material. A skeleton with a high theoretical strength is no good if in fact it buckles and collapses before it is stretched to the theoretical limit. Even so, calculations have shown that if bony endoskeletons were spread out thinly as exoskeletons they would still be stronger but, because of this tendency to buckle, not very much stronger. However, there are other disadvantages in having an exoskeleton. First, if the skeleton is at all stiff there is the necessity for periodic moulting as the animal grows. For small land animals this is difficult but larger ones, unsupported by skeleton, would collapse under their own weight and would then harden to produce an animal like a great tough pancake. Secondly, exoskeletons are very sensitive to impact, and large objects are more affected by impacts than small ones. This tends to limit the size of animals with exoskeletons. To see why this is so let us imagine an animal with the unlikely but convenient shape of a cube. It has sides of length L, and a density ρ. It runs into a wall, and is brought to rest with an acceleration a. What will be the stress on the face that hits the wall? Mass, $M = \rho L^3$. Force, $F = M.a$, therefore $F = L^3 \rho a$. The stress is proportional to the force divided by the cross-sectional area

$$\sigma = F/A = F/L^2$$

$$\text{Therefore} \quad \sigma = L^3 \rho a / L^2$$

$$\sigma = L \rho a$$

Now animals have much the same density, and therefore if two of these animals of different body length L had this accident, the stresses caused by it would be proportional to the value of L. So, even if we assume that animals all travel at the same speed, and are therefore subjected to the same accelerations, it is disadvantageous to be big if you are to be loaded in impact. Therefore our hypothetical vertebrate with a thin exoskeleton would probably be punctured by blows that on skin and muscle would merely produce painful bruises. Thirdly, the probability of buckling is raised well above its theoretical value by any notches or scratches on the element. But heavy animals exert much greater forces on their own surfaces, through contact with the ground and so on, than do light ones, so a large animal would begin seriously to weaken its exoskeleton as soon as it moved around after moulting.

All in all it seems that exoskeletons are suitable for small active animals, particularly as these often have problems with water loss, which exoskeletons ease. Large active animals like vertebrates, were they to have exoskeletons of bone, would be punctured and scored so often as to make their skeletons useless, even if they were able to moult sucessfully.

1.4 Slender elements

Although the stress produced in an element by an axial force is notionally P/A, if the element is slender it may collapse before P/A reaches the ultimate strength of the material. Think of a long thin column compressed axially. There is bound to be some slight departure from straightness, so the 'axial' force will have a slight bending moment round the middle of the column, and so produce a tendency for the column to bend into a bow. Because the column is long the bowing will produce an increase in the bending moment of the axial force, which will increase the bowing, and so on. Eventually the stiffness of the material of the column will probably prevent any more bowing, but it may not. This is the kind of collapse you can induce in a bamboo pole by pushing on one end with the other end on the floor. The load at which a slender element will collapse under axial compressive loading is given by $P = (\pi^2 E.I)/L^2$, where L is the length. Notice that in this formula the *strength* of the material does not matter, but its *stiffness* does. For this reason very long slender elements are not popular if they are to be loaded in compression. An apparent exception are the arm bones of the gibbon whose elements are slender and would collapse at quite a low load in compression. But of course, in this brachiating animal they are rarely loaded heavily in compression.

1.5   Size

In land animals the skeleton imposes quite sharp limits on size. We have already seen how the danger from impacts increases with size. Let us now imagine another situation. Suppose we have a cylindrical element of length L, bearing in the middle a load W, whose mass is proportional to the mass of the body. The maximum stress caused by the load is given by $W.L.R./4.I$. Now W will increase as the third power of the linear dimensions, while L and R will increase as the first power. What about I? As we saw before, $I = \sum y^2 \delta A$. The y^2 part will, of course increase as the square of the linear dimensions, but so also will the area of each little bit, so I will increase as the fourth power of the linear dimensions. So, in the formula giving the maximum stress, above, the part above the line will vary as the fifth power, and the part below as the fourth power of the linear dimensions. Therefore the maximum stress will be proportional to the linear dimensions. Since the *quality* of the material does not change, either safety factors must be reduced, or else the animal must change shape, and the elements of the skeleton become relatively more massive. This increase in massiveness is seen in the graviportal limbs of elephants, rhinoceroses, hippopotamuses and many dinosaurs. Such limitations do not apply in quite the same way to water-living animals, because although the mass of the body increases its weight does not. Animals as big as whales could not possibly live out of water.

1.6   The shape of elements

We have so far considered limb elements simply as cylinders with hollow centres. Of course really they interact in a very complex way with the muscles attached to them, and sometimes the function of these muscles is mainly to prevent the bending stresses in the elements becoming too great. When the weight of a man is borne by one leg only, as in running, the femur is in an awkward situation. The weight of the body, acting through the acetabulum, produces a bending load on the femur, tending to bow it outwards. However, the ilio-tibial tract, a strip of muscles and tendon, runs from the pelvis to the top of the tibia (Fig. 1–4) and its muscles on contraction tend to bow the femur inwards. These two bending tendencies to a large extent cancel each other out. Although the axial load the femur has to bear is increased by the contraction of the ilio-tibial tract muscles, the greatest stresses it has to bear are sharply reduced by its action.

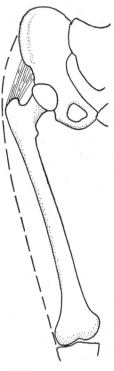

Fig. 1–4 Diagram showing the relationship between the femur and the iliotibial tract (broken line) in man. The muscles that run from the pelvis to the great trochanter on the femur are shown by fine lines. These muscles prevent the pelvis rotating round the head of the femur when the weight is on one leg only.

In fact much recent research is showing that muscles act very frequently to prevent bones being loaded in bending, and often the force of the muscles is much greater than the loads imposed on the bones by body weight. In the early days of electroconvulsive therapy patients occasionally fractured both their femora as the muscles round the top of the femora contracted under the influence of an electric shock. The stabilising effect of muscles on bones is a complex matter that is only now beginning to be worked out.

Bones have a fairly complicated internal structure. The middle section of the shaft tends to be quite thick-walled. Towards the ends of the bone the walls become thinner and then right at the end the bone expands to accommodate the bearing surfaces of the joints and the many insertions of ligaments and muscles concerned with joint action. The bone underneath the surface of the expanded ends is not solid, and is called cancellous bone. It is a delicate tracery of trabeculae, small filaments of bone that together have a rather foam-like appearance (Fig. 1–5). Although they look delicate, they are very nicely orientated to take the forces that act on the ends of the bone. Many of the shorter bones, like the ankle bones and the vertebrae are hardly more than a very thin shell of solid bone surrounding foamy cancellous bone.

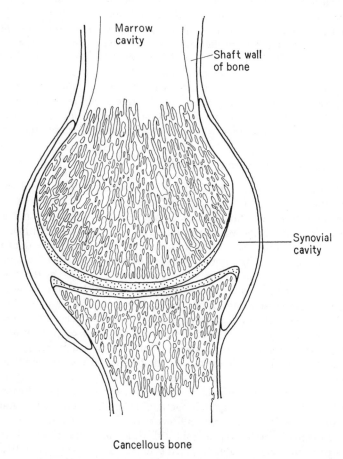

Fig. 1–5 Diagram of a longitudinal section of the ends of two articulating bones, showing how the expanded ends are filled with cancellous bone and covered with cartilage (stippled) and lie in a synovial cavity.

At first sight it seems somewhat strange that the middle of the shafts of long bones do not have a larger diameter and consequently a larger moment of inertia than they in fact do. The torque produced by torsion is as great in the middle of the bone as at the end, and bending moments produced by impacts and so on are likely to be greater in the middle of the bone than at the ends. However, the torque produced by the muscles moving the limbs is at its greatest at the ends, and declines towards the middle; to a large extent the decrease in the moment of inertia reflects this. The expansion of the ends also allows space for the large area of the synovial joint surfaces, particularly in the very mobile joints.

The elements of arthropods are more uniform along their length, and in fact tend to be fattest in the middle. But, since the muscles are inside the skeleton, this may be explained by the need to accommodate the bellies of the muscles. The muscles are rather restricted in their movements, and to ease this there are many apodemes. These are plate-like internal expansions of the cuticle. Muscles attach to them and are able to get a better purchase on them than they would on the restricted area of the internal surface of cylindrical elements. At each moult the muscles have to come unstuck from the apodemes, which are moulted with the rest of the cuticle.

1.7   The skeleton as an energy store

When an elastic object is distorted by a force the work done on the object is stored in it as *strain energy*, and the object exerts a force that tends to restore it to its unstrained state. This principle is quite often made use of by animals, particularly the arthropods, and I shall give an example here. Study of the flea has shown that, in order to jump the height it does with the small legs it has, the power required to accelerate it is much greater than can be supplied by the muscles concerned. That is to say the muscles cannot work at the necessary *rate*. Figure 1–6 shows how this is resolved. 'A', the main muscle concerned, contracts causing the femur to rotate a little, anti-clockwise, until it comes against a stop and can rotate no more. But during the jump the femur has to rotate clockwise. 'A' continues to contract, pulling the femur, and with it the pleuron and coxa, up towards the notum, and in doing so distorts a pad of resilin 'R'. Resilin is a rubbery protein. This whole contraction can take place quite slowly. When the animal is ready to jump muscle 'B' comes into action and pulls the tendon of 'A' to the other side of the hinge joining the trochanter and femur to the coxa. Now, if the coxa moves downwards the femur can rotate clockwise, and all 'A' has to do is to hold stiff while the resilin releases its strain energy in returning to the unstrained state. This it does very rapidly, and the femur is forced to rotate very rapidly also. So the muscle can work quite slowly, and give its energy of contraction to a pad of resilin, which then gives it back to the femur very quickly.

1.8   The skeleton as a protection

The skeletons of animals often act as a protection, as well as allowing muscles to act on the environment. The protection may not only be against blows from the outside, but also against stresses caused by the animal itself. For instance, violent motion of the head in man would distort the

Plate 1 (*above*) Electron micrograph of a replica of the broken surface of a coral *Pocillopora damicornis*. The individual blocks of aragonite, some of which are seen here adhering to the replica, are about 1·5 μm long. (Courtesy of S. A. Wainwright.)

Plate 2 (*below*) Electron micrograph of developing bone. The apatite needles are embedded in a matrix of collagen, and the typical banding pattern of collagen can be made out in places. Note that the apatite needles tend to be orientated in the same direction as the collagen. The needles are about 4·5 nm across, and longer than they appear here because they pass out of the plane of the section. (Courtesy of A. Ascenzi.)

This page shows various bivalve mollusc shells.

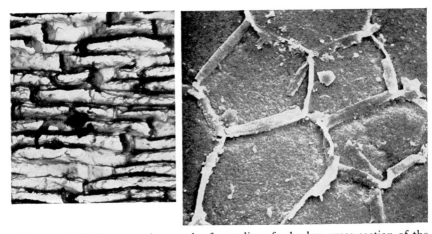

Plate 3 (*left*) Electron micrograph of a replica of a broken cross-section of the nacreous layer of *Margaritifera margaritifera*. This clearly shows the 'bricks and mortar' effect. The aragonite prisms are about $\frac{1}{2}$ μm from top to bottom.

Plate 4 (*right*) Scanning electron micrograph of the surface of the prismatic layer of *Pinctada margaritifera*. Prismatic structure consists of long prisms wrapped up in conchiolin. The top left hand prism is about 20 μm across.

Plate 5 (*left*) Scanning electron micrograph of the fractured surface of a crossed lamellar region of *Barbatia helblingi*. Several sheets can be seen, and each one is composed of a mass of smaller sheets arranged at an angle to the main sheets. The main sheets are about 2 μm across.

Plate 6 (*right*) Electron micrograph of a replica of the inner surface of the foliated layer of *Ostrea hyotis*. Foliated sheets are built up from separate lath-shaped crystals joined side-to-side to form overlapping sheets. The larger laths are about 2 μm across.

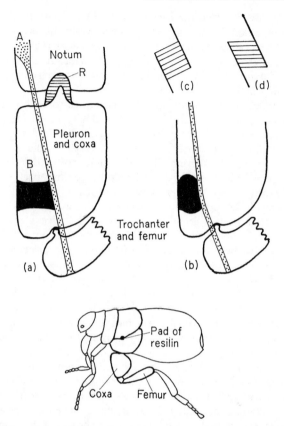

Fig. 1–6 The flea's jump. (a) and (b) are diagrammatic side views of the leg of the flea. In (a) the muscle '*A*' contracts and through its tendon causes the femur to rotate anticlockwise. This pulls the coxa and pleuron (here shown as a single block) up towards the notum, distorting the pad of resilin '*R*'. In (b) the muscle '*B*' contracts pulling the tendon over to the other side of the hinge. (c) and (d) are diagrammatic front views of the resilin pad, showing how it is distorted in shear as the muscle '*A*' contracts. (e) is a diagram of a flea, showing the relationship of the parts to each other.

brain considerably were it not firmly wrapped up in the skull. In the vertebrates, which typically have endoskeletons, mammals, birds and amphibians do not have very protective skeletons except for the skull though armadillos, for instance, have a covering of bony plates. However, fish and many reptiles often have bony scales, and external skeletons were massive in the primitive fossil fish.

The exoskeletons of arthropods inevitably act as a protection though often, as discussed before, the animal would probably be damaged less if the soft tissues protected the hard ones! Many animals develop spines as a protection, either to make themselves unapproachable, as in sea urchins, or difficult to swallow, as for instance the long spines sticking out fore and aft from delicate crab larvae and many protozoans. In some cases spines also act as flotation devices, preventing the animals from sinking too rapidly through the water.

Most sessile animals either bury themselves in the substrate or build tubes or shells round themselves. Tubes are usually secreted from the body or are made by cementing together sand grains and similar objects. They are not part of the animal itself. Shells are usually considered to be part of the animal, though non-living. Basically shells are of three main types. First, they can be box or tube-like, the animal sticking itself out to do its feeding. If the animal is threatened by a sudden shadow or similar stimulus it retreats inside its tube or box and often pulls an operculum, a kind of trap door, after itself. Secondly, the animal can have a shell with two valves, hinged in one place. The animal draws water into the cavity between the valves and filters food from it. It does not protrude much and if threatened simply draws the two valves together. This is employed by the ostracods, bivalve molluscs and the brachiopods. Thirdly, there are the snails and many cephalopod molluscs. These carry their shell around, and may or may not close an operculum after themselves if threatened.

Many shells can be described mathematically quite simply by pretending that you have a 'generating curve', say a circle, that rotates round an axis as the shell grows. One then considers three factors. How much *bigger* does the generating curve become each time it completes a revolution round the axis (the expansion rate). How does the *distance* between the centre of the generating curve and the axis alter with each revolution (the radial displacement). How far does the generating curve move *along* the axis during each rotation (the translation rate). Figure 1–7 shows this diagrammatically. The interesting thing is how restricted real animals are among the possible combinations of these three factors. Snails have a low expansion rate, a wide variety of translation rates, and a fair variety of radial displacements. The bivalve molluscs have little translation or radial displacement but a wide variety of expansion rates. The empty spaces on the block diagram are occupied by hypothetical shells of shapes not particularly well adapted for any special way of life. Describing shell shape mathematically and drawing block diagrams like this enables one to think about shells in a way that would be difficult without such formulation. Snails, for instance, have only one valve and therefore if they had a large expansion rate the mouth of the shell would be very large in relation to the total body volume, leaving much of the body unprotected. (Limpets are an exception because they use the surface of the rock to which they cling as another valve). Snail shells often have a high translation rate because this is a convenient way of producing a globular shell, which is easier to balance and carry around than a disc-shaped shell.

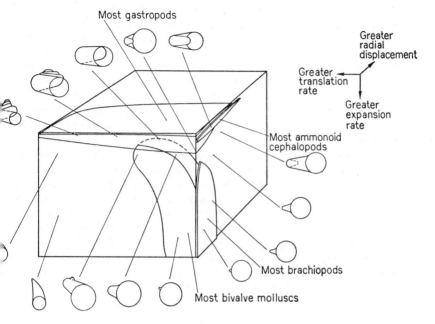

Fig. 1–7 Block diagram showing the shapes that are produced by giving a circular generating curve various expansion and translation rates, and various radial displacements. The four great groups of shelled animals: gastropods, bivalves, ammonites and brachiopods, tend to occupy well defined parts of the block. (From RAUP, D. M., *J. Palaeont.* **40,** 5, 1184).

The mechanical properties of shells are little understood. The mathematical treatment of the strength of shells is extremely awkward, and even so most normal engineering considerations are probably irrelevant. This is because unlike the skeletons of very mobile animals shells are mainly a protection against teeth. When a predator appears shelled animals can only shut up and hope for the best. Animals staying in one place can be massive, of course, and some shells are very heavy. On the other hand making a shell is an operation requiring considerable metabolic energy and time, so animals will not make their shells unnecessarily massive. In fact most shells are not very massive. If the prey is, say, 100 times smaller than the predator, then the massiveness of the shell needed to prevent it from being eaten would involve a high metabolic cost relative to the mass of the animal. It would probably be better to spend the energy building a light shell to protect the animal against the common, smaller predators, and spend the rest of the energy in producing offspring before getting caught by the fairly uncommon large predator. The production of the shell of the common snail *Cepaea nemoralis* must be a fair metabolic drain on the animal.

It is not massive enough to prevent the snail being eaten by a determined thrush or rat, but smaller animals cannot cope with it. This compromise is probably quite a successful one, as in an average habitat and year perhaps a third of all adult snails that die are eaten by these and larger predators. If all were killed in this way, probably the shell would have to be made thick enough to resist some of these attacks; on the other hand, if none were so killed, one would suspect that the snails had produced a shell with too large a safety factor. Not all breaks are from predators, however. An example of the results of natural hazards is seen in bivalve molluscs inhabiting streams and rivers. Those living high up in rocky torrents have thick shells to protect them from stones hurled about by the stream. In the more placid downstream waters the shells are usually much thinner.

In Ireland whelks have been shown to have thick or thin shells according to the amount of wave action where they live. Where the water is rough the crabs that normally eat the whelks cannot survive, and the whelks' shells are thin. They expend the saved metabolic energy on making a larger foot with which they cling on the rocks. Such thin-shelled whelks cannot survive in quieter water, because they are eaten by the crabs. Conversely, the thick-shelled whelks that can survive most attacks by crabs get washed off the more exposed rocks.

The Structure and Composition of 2
Skeletal Materials

2.1 The components of skeletons

There are in animals quite an array of structures and compositions of skeletal materials. The significance of some of the differences is obvious, but others remain baffling. We can impose some order on the variation by considering what is the organic component of the skeleton, what the inorganic or mineral, how much there is of each, and how they are put together.

Three minerals dominate the scene. In decreasing order of abundance in skeletons they are calcium carbonate $CaCO_3$ (which is found usually as calcite or aragonite, two different crystal forms of the same compound), calcium phosphate $Ca_3(PO_4)_2$ or some variant of it, and silica SiO_2. Calcium and silicon are obvious choices, being distributed widely. Phosphate is more surprising because it is often not at all common in the environment. It has in fact been suggested that bone, whose mineral is basically calcium phosphate, started in the early fishes not primarily as a mechanical skeleton but as a temporary store for phosphate for use in metabolic processes when it became scarce in the sea at certain times of the year.

The organic components of skeletons are usually proteins or polysaccharides. The proteins are fibrous and often several polypeptide chains are twisted together like the strands in a rope. The commonest, in terms of the number of animal groups in which it occurs, is the collagen type of protein. This is a somewhat vague term, and refers to proteins that react to various chemical and physical tests in a particular way; collagens are fairly similar. Typical collagen, such as is found in bone, tendon and skin has a simple primary structure. (The primary structure of a protein is simply a list of the amino acids, starting at one end and going to the other). There are many glycine units and there is also a high proportion of the rare amino acid hydroxyproline. Collagen is arranged in a rope-like triple helix (not to be confused with the double helix of DNA or the alpha helix of many enzyme proteins). There are in collagen few amino acids with large side groups, and this allows the chains to come very close together, and bind together at regular intervals. As a result the chains have little tendency to slip past one another if they are pulled and collagen is very strong in tension though, because its fibres are not stiff, it can be bent easily.

Keratin, found principally in the claws, hair, horn and skin of tetrapod vertebrates is another fibrous protein with a rope-like structure. Much of its strength comes from cystine linkages or disulphide bridges, binding one

(a)

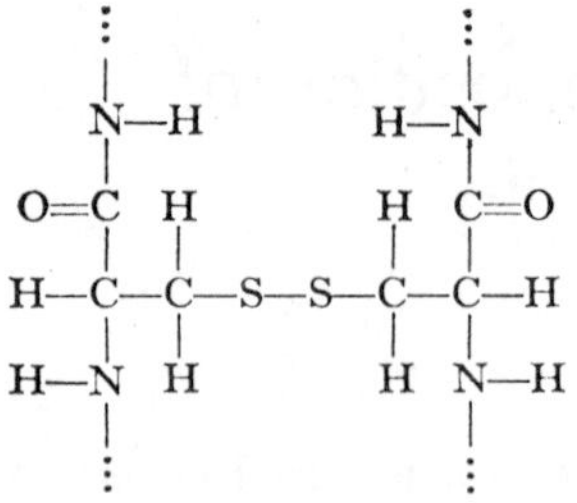

(b)

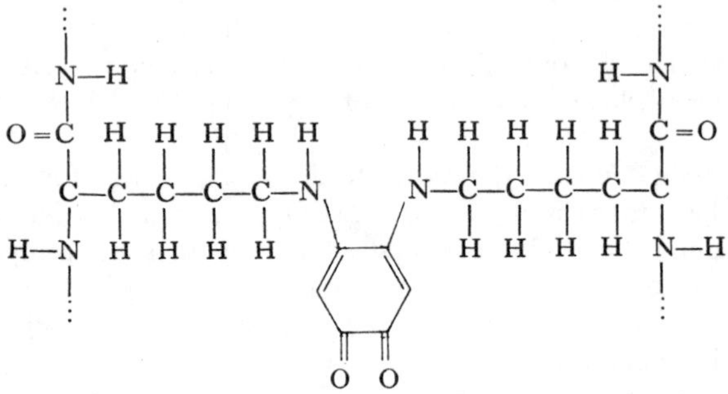

(c)

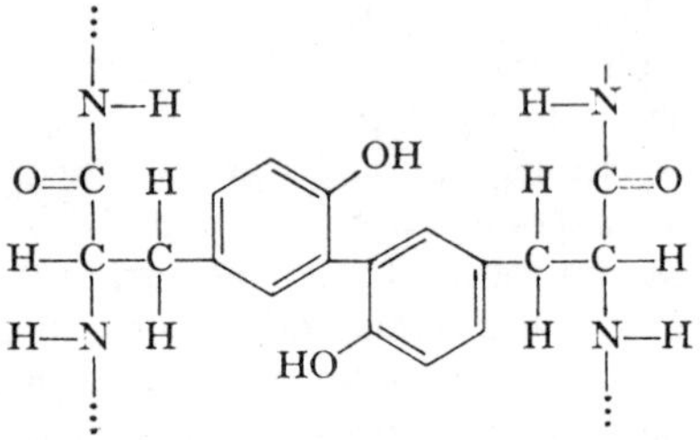

(d)

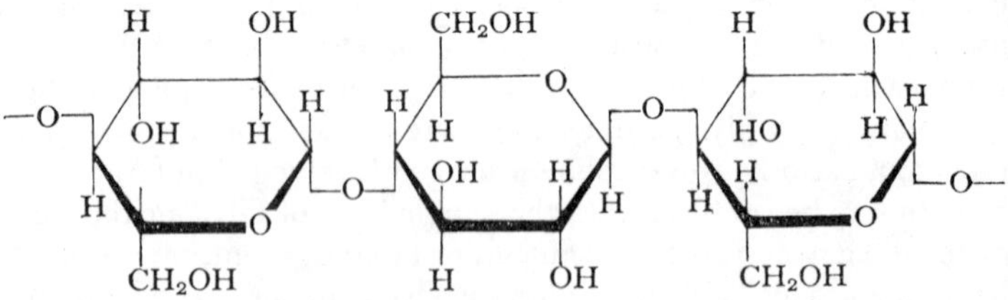

(e)

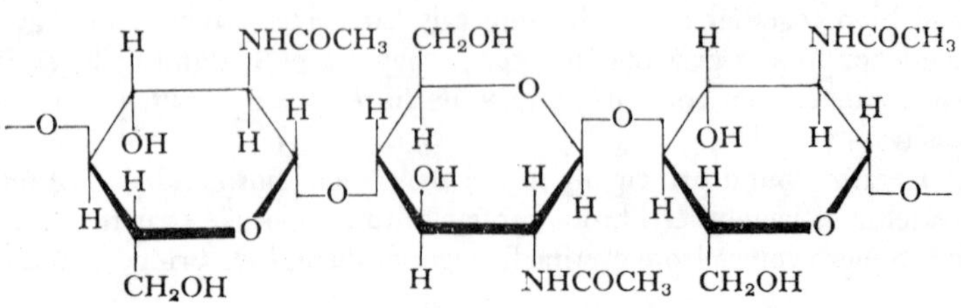

chain to the next through two sulphur atoms (Fig. 2–1(a)). Silks, another group of fibrous proteins, have a skeletal function outside the body. They are unusual in being composed mainly of glycine, alanine and serine. These simple amino acids have small side groups, allowing the separate chains to come very close together so that hydrogen bonding can take place easily. The animal spinning the silk has protein chains jumbled up inside silk glands in a viscous liquid form. On leaving the body the silk is extruded through a small hole and stretched. This aligns all the molecules alongside each other, and almost instantly so much hydrogen bonding takes place that it is effectively irreversible. This change from a liquid to a strong fibre without the use of complicated enzyme systems is of course a great help to animals needing to produce a great length of stable fibre very quickly. There are other mechanical proteins, particularly in arthropods, but their structure is less well-known.

In general proteins are rather soluble and there is no system to hold a large number of separate chains together. This means that they are useless as mechanical fibres. However, the slipping apart of the chains can be prevented by covalent bonding between them, usually with an aromatic compound as a link. The linking of proteins in this way is called *tanning*. An example is the quinone tanning very often present in arthropod cuticular proteins (Fig. 2–1(b)). It has of course the same function as the cystine link but the tanned links are longer and more flexible than disulphide bridges.

Polysaccharides, many simple sugars joined together in long chains, have among their members the most abundant skeletal material on earth: cellulose. This is characteristic of plants, and is composed of many molecules of glucose. A polysaccharide is very important in animals also, in the form of chitin. This is chemically rather like cellulose and has a very long, unbranched molecule. The repeating unit is not glucose, however, but acetylglucosamine (Fig. 2–1(e)). Chitin is widespread, particularly in arthropods.

2.2 Skeletal materials in different groups

Having considered the kinds of constituents we are likely to find in animal skeletons, we can now consider the groups of animals in turn.

Protozoa. Many protozoa have skeletons of some kind (Fig. 2–2). The radiolarians usually have delicate spicules of silica. The foraminifera are

Fig. 2–1 (*opposite*) Structure of some organic skeletal materials. Three methods of linking two chains of proteins together. (a) Cystine link, or disulphide bridge, as in keratin. (b) Quinone tanning, as in arthropod scleroproteins. (c) Biphenyl link, as in resilin. Two skeletal polysaccharides. (d) Structure of the repeating units of cellulose. (e) Structure of the repeating units of chitin.

often enclosed by shells of calcium carbonate, usually calcite, or they may cement together tiny grains of siliceous sand. The enormous deposits of chalk in the world contain large quantities of the skeletons of foraminiferans. The calcite seems to be deposited in a delicate matrix of protein. Not all protozoa make use of such conventional materials. For instance, some foraminiferans make use of grains of barium sulphate and, most bizarre of all, some radiolarians have a skeleton of strontium sulphate.

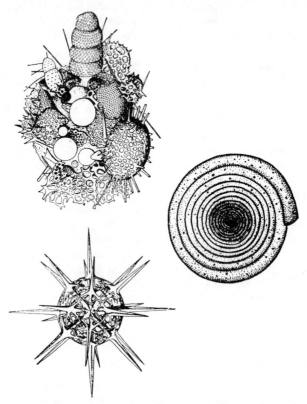

Fig. 2–2   Hard skeletons of various protozoans. One is made by cementing together bits of skeletons from other protozoans.

Sponges. The sponges have a very simple organization but they can grow quite large and need skeletons to keep themselves intact and to hold open their orifices and internal cavities. Some have skeletons of calcium carbonate needles, some of a horny collagen-like protein called spongin, some of silica in spicules, and some of a mixture of the last two. The horny sponge of the demospongiae was the old bathroom sponge before plastics were introduced. Probably the spicular skeletons are useful in making the sponges unattractive to browsers, and the horny skeleton allows considerable distortion without damage. However, it is strange that within a group of animals quite closely related to each other such extremely different skeletal materials should be used (Fig. 2–3).

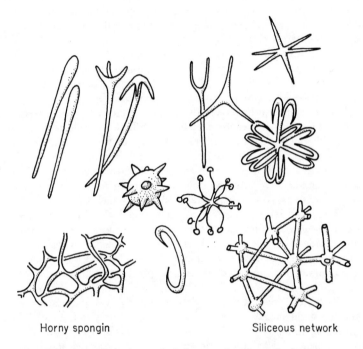

Horny spongin   Siliceous network

Fig. 2–3 Spicules and skeletons of various sponges.

Cnidaria. The cnidaria known to most students of biology in temperate climates are fairly insignificant ecologically. In the tropics cnidaria form the basis for one of the richest habitats in the world: coral. The colonial coral groups, mainly the scleractinians, secrete a calcium carbonate base to support and protect themselves. It is secreted on the outside of the animals, and when the animals die new ones secrete their skeletons on the old; in this way the coral grows massive. Coral-forming animals cannot live below a depth of about 40 metres, below which their green symbionts cannot function effectively. Nevertheless coral islands have been found in which the depth of the coral rock is much greater than this. Darwin suggested, and this has been backed up by later work, that the great depth must have been caused by the corals managing to keep pace with a slow change in the water level. Probably the water level rose after the last glaciation in the pleistocene.

In the scleractinian corals the main skeletal component is aragonite, but there is a very small amount of organic material in the form of chitinous threads between the crystals. These stony corals are brittle, and get their strength by growing massive (Plate 1). Among the gorgonacean corals, although calcium carbonate is the usual skeletal component, many species have·nearly 100 per cent of a collagenous protein called gorgonin. In some, such as *Isis* the 'stems' of the colonies are composed alternately of coloured gorgonin and aragonite, giving a neapolitan ice cream effect. This enables the stem to move in response to the pounding of the waves. In the sea fans the skeleton is almost 100 per cent gorgonin. These corals are flexible, and can expose a broad, flat, but thin surface to the currents. Such an arrangement would not be possible for a stony coral.

Obelia and many other hydroids have a chitinous *perisarc* covering the body, and in some species this may have a stiffening of calcareous deposits.

Wormlike lower invertebrates. The majority of the lower invertebrates, such as flatworms, the nematodes and the nemertea, are wormlike and use no really hard skeletal parts though some, like the oligochaete and polychaete annelids, have bristles of chitin or tanned protein. Some, like the serpulid annelids, secrete hard calcite tubes in which they live.

Bryozoa. These are very small, colonial animals that live on seaweed and rock. They secrete complicated tubes and cases round themselves and we shall consider how these work later. The skeletons are variable in composition, usually having a fair amount of calcite, but there is always some organic matter present, which is a chitin-protein mixture, and in fact the whole covering of the animal may be organic.

Molluscs. The molluscs's shell is their most obvious characteristic and it shows a great variety of external form: one has only to think of a limpet, a garden snail, an oyster and a cuttlefish to realise this. Usually there is a layer of protein called the periostracum on the outside, and inside this there is calcite or aragonite mixed with a small amount of protein called conchiolin. The protein has a high proportion of glycine and alanine, as in fibrous proteins generally. Calcite has hexagonal symmetry, is more stable and is less soluble than aragonite, which has rhombic symmetry. Which of the two forms of calcium carbonate crystallizes out depends on the particular circumstances of the crystallization. Many organic and inorganic ions can influence the result and it is closely controlled by the mollusc. A single shell may have layers of both crystal forms arranged in a way quite characteristic of all individuals of the species, and quite different from the pattern in the next species. There is considerable variety in the detailed relationship between the protein and mineral components. For instance, in the *nacreous* or pearly type one can see in cross section under the electron microscope a picture like a brick wall, with crystals of aragonite wrapped up in sheets of conchiolin (Plate 3). In the *prismatic* type there are typically polygonal columnar blocks, looking rather like the famous basalt blocks of the Giant's Causeway. Each prism is separated from its neighbours by a thick conchiolin wall. The prisms are arranged at right angles to the wall of the shell, unlike the nacreous type in which the bricks lie parallel to the surface (Plate 4). In the *crossed lamellar* structure there are interdigitating sheets, each one of which is made up of a mass of crystals lying at an angle to the main sheet, and the organic matter is not at all obvious (Plate 5). In various species of mollusc the shell varies from about 0·01 per cent to 5 per cent organic matter in the dried shell. Although the differences between the different groups of molluscs are very characteristic and constant, they are not well understood in terms of any mechanical or developmental requirements of the different groups. The shells of cephalopods are of the usual molluscan composition unless they become very reduced. The 'bone' of the cuttlefish has about 5 per cent organic matter, but the squid has reduced its internal shell to nothing but a horny shield.

Arthropods. The skeleton of arthropods is mechanically and in many other ways extremely adaptable, and has undoubtedly helped greatly in the arthropods' success. We shall consider first the insect cuticle. It is shown diagramatically in Fig. 2–4. On the outside is a thin epicuticle. This has a

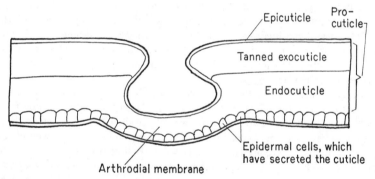

Fig. 2–4   Cross section of an insect cuticle. This diagram shows how the cuticle is thin and remains untanned in places, such as arthrodial membranes, where flexibility is required.

base of protein, usually tanned, above this there is a layer of wax, and finally there may be a thin varnish-like layer. The main function of the epicuticle is to keep the surface of the insect waterproof. Beneath the epicuticle is the procuticle, the thick layer of the cuticle. It is a protein-chitin mixture, the chitin fibres being embedded in a protein matrix. The proportions vary, but usually there is rather more protein than chitin. There are many proteins, for instance in one insect at least a dozen different ones have been distinguished. Always quite a large part of this protein is firmly bound to the chitin, probably by covalent bonds. The protein has a tendency to become tanned, usually by aromatic molecules such as quinone. This tanning rarely extends the whole thickness of the cuticle and the outer, tanned, part is called the exocuticle, while the inner, untanned, part is called the endo-cuticle. The thickness of the cuticle, the amount of tanning, and the relative amounts of chitin and protein can all be varied. As a result the cuticle can be very hard, as in the mandibles, or it can be soft and pliable, as in arthrodial membranes covering joints.

When looked at under the microscope the cuticle is seen to be made up of a series of layers, rather like plywood. The direction of the chitin fibres changes through the thickness of the layer. Typically each layer has a series of planes, with the orientation of the chitin in one plane slightly different from those on each side. Any small thickness of cuticle, therefore, has chitin fibrils pointing in all directions in the plane of the cuticle. This obviously could have great mechanical importance. Insects also make great use of the rubbery protein resilin, which has been mentioned already and will be discussed again. The cuticle of other arthropods is similar to that of insects. The principal differences lie in the relative amount of the tanned and the untanned protein, and the presence or absence of calcium carbon-ate. In the onycophorans, a group of very primitive arthropods (or ad-vanced annelids), for instance, the proportion of protein is very great and it is not tanned. This makes the cuticle very pliant and flexible, allowing the onycophorans to squeeze into very small crevices. In many of the crustacea and millipedes the cuticle is hardened and stiffened by the de-position of calcium carbonate. It seems that in these cuticles the more calcium carbonate there is, the less protein, the amount of chitin being more or less constant.

Brachiopods. The brachiopods look like bivalve molluscs, but they are un-related to them, though they do live in a similar way by filtering food from the water. They have two valves or parts of the shell, and these valves have a great array of forms according to the habitat and particular way of life of the animals. There are two main types of shell composition. In one, the chitinophosphatic type, characteristic of most of the smaller brachiopods, there is a large amount of organic material rather like chitin. This can make up to 40 per cent of the dry weight of the shell. The mineral part is mainly calcium phosphate. The organic and mineral parts may be mixed together, or they may be separated in neat layers. In the other type, which is much more important numerically, there is only about 4 per cent of organic matter, it is protein, and the mineral is calcium carbonate. There is a fairly thin 'primary' outer layer, with very little protein, consisting of many tiny needles of calcite at right angles to the surface. Then there is a thick inner 'fibrous' layer, in which there are much larger needles of calcite separated from each other by protein sheaths, like the blocks in the prismatic layer of molluscs. The brachiopods have a rather uniform way of life, and there seems to be no obvious reason why the two groups should have such differ-ent shell constructions. There is some evidence that the earliest brachiopods had an almost entirely organic skeleton, and that the addition of calcium phosphate or carbonate came later (Fig. 2–5).

Echinoderms. These animals, the starfish, sea urchins and their relatives, have a most unusual skeleton. It is made of calcite-like crystal, but with magnesium taking the place of some of the calcium. In natural rocks magnesium carbonate is found with calcium carbonate, but either more or less of it than is found in echinoderms. The echinoderm skeleton seems to be mineralogically unstable, and fossils usually lose some of their magnesium, which is replaced by calcium. What advantage it is to have a skeleton made of a crystal that is somewhat difficult to make and maintain is unknown. There is virtually no organic matrix in the mineral. There is still debate on this point, some people saying there is a substantial protein matrix. In my opinion this is not correct. The skeleton, instead of being solid, is

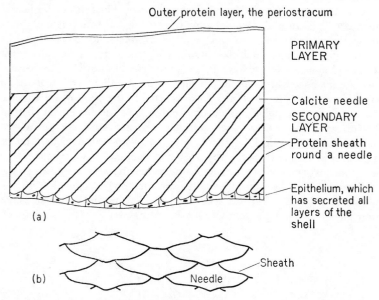

Fig. 2-5 (a) Diagram of the cross section of a calcitic brachiopod shell. (b) Cross section of some needles, showing their characteristic shape, which is determined by their protein sheaths.

pierced by many interconnecting holes (Plate 7). This is called the 'stereom'. In life the holes are filled with living soft tissue. The skeleton is made of separate pieces, each of which can be an inch or more long and, in the case of spines, several inches. Nevertheless each behaves according to the ordinary mineralogical tests as if it were a single crystal. The pieces do not *look* like crystals, because they are full of holes and have whatever shape is required by the animal. The separate pieces are strapped together by collagen fibres which loop through the channels in the calcite like laces through eyelets.

Vertebrates. The vertebrates have developed two very different kinds of skeletal material, both based on calcium phosphate. These are bone and enamel. Bone is essentially phosphates of calcium laid down in a matrix of collagen fibrils. There are other substances present, notably water, citrate, some protein-polysaccharide complexes and some other protein. The rest of bone is phosphate of calcium. Much work has been done on the mineral of bone, but it is a difficult substance to characterise exactly. Basically it seems to be hydroxyapatite $Ca_{10}(PO_4)_6(OH)_2$. However, there are other ions inserted here and there in the crystal lattice, and the crystal is generally imperfect. The needle-shaped apatite crystals surround and impregnate the collagen fibrils, and there is evidence that there are direct covalent bonds between the mineral and the collagen. The needles are about 4·5 nm across, and from 200 nm to indefinitely long. The collagen fibrils and their associated needles form a highly orientated structure (Plate 2). How the fibrils are arranged varies. In a type of bone called *woven bone* the collagen fibrils are tangled up more or less at random, so that any small volume of bone is likely to have fibrils pointing in all directions. In *lamellar bone* the fibrils are arranged in lamellae or sheets, about 10 μm thick. In any particular lamella the fibrils are orientated in the plane of the lamella. They also tend to point in a particular direction within the lamella but this direction can change over quite short distances (Plate 8). Woven bone is laid down quickly, particularly in embryonic life; lamellar bone is laid down in a more leisurely way. A typical mammalian long bone would have much woven bone in the foetus, but as new bone is laid down on the outside to make the bone bigger the woven bone is eroded from the middle. Eventually only lamellar bone may be left but, if the erosion is not even all the way round, some woven bone may be left (Fig. 2–6(a)–(c).

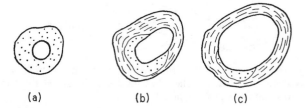

(a)   (b)   (c)

Fig. 2–6 Diagram of the cross section of a long bone, showing how during development (**a–c**) woven bone is replaced by lamellar bone. Woven bone dotted, lamellar bone lines.

Bone is rigid and cannot expand, so any growth or change of shape has to take place either by the laying down of new bone on a pre-existing surface or by the erosion of bone from a pre-existing surface.

Textbooks usually give undue weight to Haversian systems, or secondary osteones. These are cylindrical systems of concentric lamellae surrounding a cavity, the Haversian canal, which contains blood vessels and nerves. They are formed by the infilling of cylindrical cavities that have been eroded round blood vessels in the shaft wall of bones (Fig. 2–7). The erosion of the cavity probably serves the function of destroying and replacing dead bone, and also of releasing calcium or phosphate into the bloodstream when it is needed. The weight given to secondary osteones as a feature of bone is undue because although they are a prominent feature of the bones of man and some larger carnivores, they are less plentiful in herbivores, and are virtually absent in small mammals. In non-mammalian vertebrates they appear in some fossil reptiles, some birds, but hardly anywhere else.

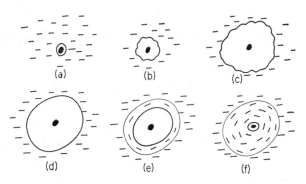

Fig. 2–7   The formation of a Haversian system. (**a**) A blood vessel running in a channel in the bone, shown in cross section. (**b**) An erosion cavity forms round it. (**c**) The cavity increases in size. (**d**) The surface is smoothed off. (**e**) New bone is laid down on the surface. (**f**) The Haversian system is complete.

Bone is living unlike, say, a snail shell, because it is full of bone cells called osteocytes. These live entombed in cavities called lacunae, and they have tenuous connections with their neighbouring cells through very slender cytoplasmic processes extending through tiny tubes called canaliculi. Each osteocyte has direct or indirect connection with one of the many blood vessels that permeate bone. Even so, osteocytes in patches of bone may die; and the lacunae become empty. Bone without bone cells may persist indefinitely, but it does show a tendency to become overmineralised, and if this happens the bone becomes very brittle (Plates 9 and 10).

The bone of vertebrates other than mammals is fairly like mammalian bone though there is a tendency in the more sluggish vertebrates for there to be a much less rich blood supply. The most advanced fishes, the teleosts, show a peculiar specialisation in that their bone is without osteocytes. The significance of this is unknown, although it is known that this acellular bone is very bad at healing fractures, in fact they simply don't heal. But this cannot be a direct consequence of the lack of cells because osteocytes do not play a very active part in bone healing.

Dentine, which underlies the enamel in teeth, is very like bone in many respects. The relationship between the collagen fibrils and the apatite is the same, but the arrangement of the cells is different. When bone grows the cells that are to become osteocytes lie against the edge of the growing bone and then bone is laid down outside them. In dentine the dentinal cells also lie up against the growing edge. Instead of being incorporated, however, they retreat before the advancing edge and pay off long processes

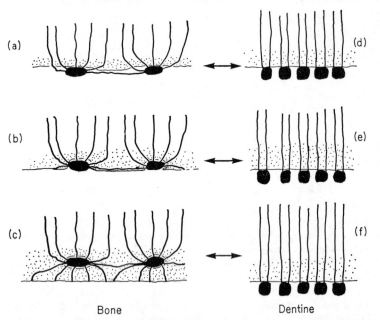

Bone   Dentine

Fig. 2–8   Comparison of growth in bone and dentine. In bone, (**a, b, c**) the cells, shown solid black, become trapped by the advancing bone. The level of the initial surface is shown by arrows. The cells connect with each other and with the free surface by canaliculi. In dentine (**d, e, f**), the cells are much closer packed on the surface. They do not get trapped but leave processes behind.

which extend right into the dentine. So, although there are no cell bodies in dentine, there are cell processes. It is interesting that the bone of many primitive fish was more like dentine than bone, and the denticles in present-day shark's skin are very like teeth, having a cap of enamel covering a base of dentine (Fig. 2–8).

Enamel is the extremely hard tissue that the vertebrates have produced. Like bone its mineral is apatite, but there is much more of it, about 98 per

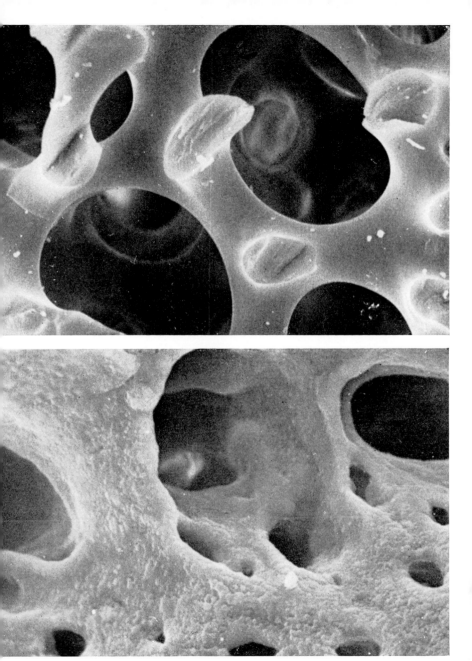

Plate 7 Scanning electron micrographs of the skeleton of the sea urchin *Echinus esculentus*. (a) *Above:* from the inside of the test. The surfaces in life would be covered with living cells, and these have kept the surface smooth. (**b**) *Below:* from an exposed part, behind the tip of a tooth. The living tissue has died back, and the surface is much rougher. (Courtesy of D. Nichols.)

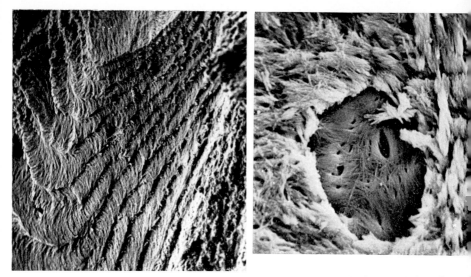

Plate 8 (*left*) Scanning electron micrograph of some obliquely fractured lamellae of Haversian system. The separate lamellae can be seen, and also the direction of the collag fibrils in each lamella. (Courtesy of A. Boyde.)

Plate 9 (*right*) Scanning electron micrograph of an osteocyte lacuna. This lacuna was the process of forming, and is viewed from the still unossified part of the tissue. The s tissue, including the osteocyte itself and much collagen, has been removed. The openings the canaliculi can be seen. The lacuna is about 11 μm across at its widest. (Courtesy A. Boyde.)

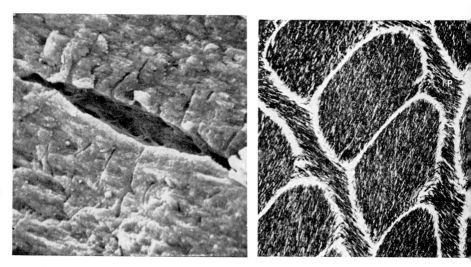

Plate 10 (*left*) Scanning electron micrograph of an osteocyte, broken across its midd The lacuna is much narrower in one plane than in the two others. The openings of t canaliculi can be seen, and also in places the course of the canaliculi can be seen on t fractured surface. The lacuna is about 3·5 μm across the widest part of the shorter axis. (Co tesy of A. Boyde.)

Plate 11 (*right*) Electron micrograph of a cross-section of enamel. The prisms have be cut slightly obliquely. Each prism is a mass of apatite needles. The prisms are about 2 μ across. The white areas are occupied by organic material in life. In places (IP) there interprismatic areas with apatite needles between the prisms. (Courtesy of A. Boyde.)

cent of the dry weight, and the crystals are much larger than in bone. The protein is not collagen. Although many textbooks say that the protein is keratin there seems to be little evidence that this is so. The protein seems, in fact, to be special to enamel. Just as dentine is produced by a layer of cells that retreat before the advancing surface of dentine, so enamel is produced by cells that do the same. However, they do not leave any living processes within the enamel. Enamel consists of prism-shaped bundles of apatite crystals wrapped up in the protein component, looking rather like the prismatic type of mollusc shell. However, the apatite crystals are much smaller than the mineral crystals in molluscs, and also the protein extends as a diaphanous network into the mineral of the prisms themselves (Plate 11).

Another important skeletal material in vertebrates is cartilage. It is a complex substance, and rather variable. It consists of cells lying in a matrix of collagen fibres, mucopolysaccharides, and a great deal of water. Mucopolysaccharides are proteins having attached to them long chains of some kind of polysaccharide. The relative amounts of the three main components vary considerably. Cartilage is found as a kind of softer version of bone. The cartilaginous fish have endoskeletons entirely composed of cartilage, and other fish have much cartilage where one might expect bone. In many vertebrates cartilage is found in places that need to have a particular shape but which are not subjected to great loads—the nose, the external ears, the last few ribs and so on. It is also found on the bearing surfaces of joints. Cartilage can become calcified with apatite, but mechanically the result is not nearly as good as bone.

Although cartilage is mainly a vertebrate tissue it does occur in some invertebrates. For instance, cartilage supports the tentacles of many sedentary polychaetes and the horny tooth belt (the radula) of gastropods. There are cartilages in the heads of cephalopods and the gills of king crabs. These cartilages all contain collagen and mucopolysaccharides, but they never become calcified.

The Mechanical Properties of Skeletal Materials   3

We start this chapter with a table (Table 1) showing some important mechanical properties of skeletal materials and their components. The values have been taken from a number of sources and are of varying reliability. Also there is considerable variation within particular materials. If so an average value for E is given, but the highest reliable strength value is given.

Material		Specific gravity	E	Specific E	σ	Specific σ
Rubbers	Abduction	ca 1·3	4	3·1	—	—
	Elastin	ca 1·3	0·6	0·5	—	—
	Resilin	ca 1·3	1·9	1·5	3	2·3
Orientated proteins	Collagen	1·4	1000	700	500	360
	Keratin	1·3	3500	2700	200	150
	Silk	1·3	10 000	7700	500	380
Polysaccharides	Cellulose (ramie)	1·6	40 000	25 000	1000	620
	Chitin	ca 1·6	45 000	28 000	650	410
Minerals	Apatite	3·2	180 000	56 000	—	—
	Calcite	2·7	140 000	52 000	—	—
Vertebrates	Cartilage	1·1	15	14	1	1
	Tendon	1·3	190	150	100	77
	Bone	2·0	14 000	7000	180	90
	Ear Bone	2·4	31 000	13 000	—	—
	Enamel	2·6	84 000	32 000	—	—
Arthropods	Locust cuticle	1·2	9500	7900	95	79
	Carcinus (crab)	1·9	13 000	6800	34	18
Cephalopod mollusc shell	*Nautilus*	2·7	44 000	16 000	84	31
Bivalve mollusc shells	*Anodonta*	2·7	43 000	16 000	38	14
	Atrina	2·6	58 000	21 000	67	25
	Egeria	2·7	78 000	29 000	50	19
	Pinna	2·7	12 000	4400	62	23
Gastropod mollusc shells	*Patella*	2·7	68 000	25000	32	12
	Turbo	2·7	54 000	20000	108	40
Sea urchin Spine	*Centrostephanus*	2·0	7400	3700	—	—

Table 1 The mechanical properties of some skeletal materials. Values for E and ultimate tensile strength (σ) are given as meganewtons per square metre. Above the line are properties of materials that function on their own (like silk) or are associated with other materials. Below the line are the properties of materials made from combinations of other materials. Unfortunately no information exists concerning the mechanical properties of the protein of cuticle

The specific strength and the specific E are the observed values divided by the specific gravity of the material. Most skeletons, as I pointed out in Chapter 1, are the result of a compromise between the need for strength or stiffness and the need to be light. Bulk is rarely a limiting factor. Therefore among possible materials that with the highest *specific* strength or stiffness will usually be the best mechanically. It is interesting, for instance, that from this point of view cuticle seems to be almost as good a material as bone. Of course, if only a very small amount of the material is used, its weight will be unimportant. The high density of enamel, for instance, is acceptable bringing with it as it does the ability to be very hard. I do not intend to discuss the table in detail, but there are one or two points that may be mentioned. First, the range of stiffness values is much greater than the range of strength values. This means that as materials get stiffer they do not get stronger in proportion. In fact the highest strengths (in the organic fibres) are not found in the stiffest materials. Second, the tensile strength of apatite and calcite are not known, but in each case it will almost certainly be low, much lower than the strength of bone or the mollusc shells. Similarly the strength of the very stiff ear bone is unknown, but it is certainly much lower than the strength of ordinary bone. Third, the rubbers have a very low E. The reasons for these facts will be examined in this chapter.

For a skeletal material not only is static strength important, but also stiffness and resistance to impact. It is possible partially to overcome some faults in a skeletal material by good design. For instance, if the *material* is pliable, the *element* can be made rigid by increasing the second moment of area but not, of course, so far that there is a danger of local buckling. Even so, excellence in all properties of a material is not possible because some are incompatible. This is particularly true of stiffness and resistance to impact. Usually an element needs to be stiff. However, it will survive an impact only if it can absorb all the energy of the impact without any part of it reaching the breaking stress. The area under the stress/strain curve is, very roughly, proportional to the amount of energy that can be absorbed by a material before it breaks. Figure 1–2 shows that the area under the curve is larger, at a given stress, the lower the value of E. It is possible to have a high E and yet be resistant to impact by having considerable plastic deformation before fracture. But this, of course, has the disadvantage that the plastic deformation is not recovered when the stress is removed, and so the element will be deformed as a result of the impact. Even so, a small plastic region can markedly increase the energy required to fracture a material compared with that necessary if it is entirely brittle. (Brittle means showing no plastic flow before breaking, and does not necessarily imply that the material is stiff; for instance, rubber and jelly are brittle while most steels are not.)

We shall now look at the various skeletal materials, and see how their desirable properties result from their particular structure.

3.1 The stiff materials

As we have seen, the materials available to animals for skeletons are organic fibres and mineral crystals. Organic fibres are usually strong in tension but, because they are fibrous they tend to collapse by kinking if compressed. They are therefore useless on their own for building any normal skeleton that has to resist compression. Most mineral crystals, on the other hand, are very stiff indeed both in tension and compression, fairly strong in compression, very weak in tension and very very weak in impact. We must now see why crystals of mineral are so weak in tension.

If we take a mineral like calcite we can, knowing the strength, angles and distances of its chemical bonds, calculate its E. These calculated values are near enough to the experimentally determined values. However, similar calculations for the tensile strength give values that are a hundred or a thousand times higher than the experimentally determined values. The observed strength is much less than the theoretical strength because any actual crystal inevitably has tiny notches and defects in it. Although these notches are small they are very important, because they cause *stress concentrations* at their tip. A stress concentration is visualised in Fig. 3–1. In

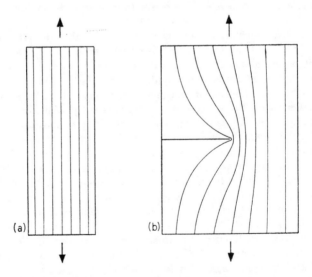

Fig. 3–1 Diagram of the stress-concentrating effect of a narrow slit in a material.

A the lines of force run straight from one end of the stressed material to the other. In *B* there is a very narrow crack, and the lines of force have to make their way round the tip. Although *A* and *B* have the same area at the narrowest place, in *B* there is a concentration of force at the crack tip, so that there the stress will be much higher than the average. Just at this place, therefore, the material may be raised to its breaking stress, and the crack start to run. For rather complicated reasons the length of the crack is important and it cannot run, no matter how sharp-ended it is, if it is too short. The crack, as it advances, still has a very sharp tip, so the stress concentration remains high. As the crack gets longer the force needed to keep it running gets less and it accelerates, and after it has travelled about a centimetre it may be travelling at several hundred metres a second. The crack will therefore run right through the material and break it in two. If a crack is just starting to run, it is obviously important, if it is to continue, that the crack tip remain sharp. Were it somehow to become blunt the stress concentration would become less and the crack might stop running. Such a situation is shown in Fig. 3–2(a)–(d). The crack R runs through the left

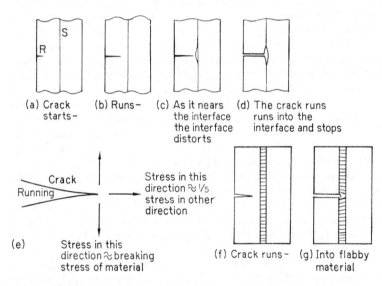

(a) Crack starts–   (b) Runs–   (c) As it nears the interface the interface distorts   (d) The crack runs runs into the interface and stops

(e)   Crack Running   Stress in this direction $\approx 1/5$ stress in other direction   Stress in this direction $\approx$ breaking stress of material   (f) Crack runs–   (g) Into flabby material

Fig. 3–2   Diagram of the blunting effects of interfaces in brittle materials.

hand side of the material, but the longitudinal crack S half way across has the effect of reducing the stress concentration to virtually nothing when R runs into it. Figure 3–2(c) shows another important thing: as R approaches S the latter opens up. This is because just in front of the running crack there is a tensile stress pulling *in the direction* of the running crack. This tensile stress has a value about one fifth of the value of the stress that is opening up the running crack (Fig. 3–2(e)). Since the latter will have a value roughly equal to the strength of the material (that is why the crack is running at all) it follows that S would open up even if it were not a crack but merely a weaker plane in the material, as long as it was not stronger than about one fifth of the tensile strength of the material as a whole. Therefore, if a material could be made of crystals, orientated with their long axes in the direction that stresses would occur in life, full of interfaces between the crystals that were less than one fifth as strong as the crystals themselves, cracks could not easily be transferred between the crystals, and the material would be much stronger in tension than it would be if it were a single crystal. The same effect would be given if the material at the interface were very pliant so that the crack running into it distorted it without breaking it, and the crack would become blunt-ended (Fig. 3-2(f) and (g)).

In effect, of course, this is how most stiff skeletal materials are arranged. Bone is a clear example. The tiny crystalline needles of apatite are all discrete but are joined to their neighbours by the collagen matrix. Because they are so small any surface flaws they may have are not long enough to be dangerous. If a needle does crack, however, the crack cannot pass through the flabby matrix, and so it does not pass through the bone. Nor is this all. Should a crack really start running it will continually be running into rather weak interfaces on a much larger scale, the interfaces between lamellae, round Haversian systems, and between laminae. It is interesting that the tensile strength of a bone tested in a direction at right angles to the long axis of the bone (a most unlikely event in life) but having the orientation of the stress running in front of a 'conventional' crack, is about 1/10 of the strength of the bone when tested along the long axis. This shows that the interfaces have almost exactly the right strength to act as crack stoppers and yet still allow the bone to cohere. It is important that the apatite needles should be long and narrow, for if they were like little spheres the crack could run through the collagen between the spheres. As it is, no crack can pass through a bone without encountering an almost infinite palisade of apatite needles, and many weak interfaces at a larger scale. The collagen also allows the needles to move relative to each other, so that the E of bone is much lower than that of apatite, but much higher than that of collagen.

Of course, in a highly orientated material like bone stresses acting across the grain will be dangerous. Lamellar bone, of which this is particularly true, is usually found only in places where it would be difficult to produce stresses in the 'wrong' direction. Woven bone, with no particular grain, will be weaker than lamellar bone in one plane, but stronger than it in others. In woven bone the load will be borne mainly by those parts that happen to have their fibres in the right direction. One can show that these parts will have a high value for E in the direction of the force as well as a high strength. Because the bone deforms as a whole, the weak parts, with a correspondingly low E, will not be stressed to dangerously high values (Fig. 3-3).

The ear bones of many mammals have a much higher mineral content and are much stiffer and weaker than ordinary bone. This does not matter for ear bones because they are not exposed to great stress, and their extra

stiffness and density have important acoustical functions. It does empha-
sise the point that the particular proportions of the organic and mineral
parts of the bone may be very important. In fact recent work shows that
the amount of mineralisation of ordinary bone (about 60 per cent by
weight) is critical, and that if it is increased by even a few per cent the
value of E increases and the impact strength begins to fall very rapidly.

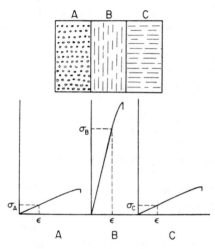

Fig. 3–3   Stresses in woven bone. **A**, **B** and **C** are three blocks of bone whose
fibres are orientated in the directions indicated. The block is pulled in tension
from top to bottom. The corresponding stress/strain curves are shown below.
The strain ϵ (which is the same for all three blocks because they are united
firmly together) and the corresponding stress σ (which is not the same) are
indicated by dotted lines.

According to Table 1 collagen is much stronger than bone, and to consider how the apatite becomes reasonably strong might seem irrelevant.
The collagen could provide the tensile strength and the apatite the compressive strength and the stiffness. There are two things to be said about
this. First, and less important, is that the strength of collagen given in
Table 1 is for a single fibril under ideal conditions. The much lower
strength of tendon, which is mainly collagen, suggests that, since the ideal
strength of a single fibril is not found when many fibrils run together, the
strength of the collagen in bone could well be low. But, secondly, even if
the strength of collagen were very high in bone it would not help the apatite because its E is so very much lower. If the collagen is subjected to a
large force it may very well be able to bear it, but in doing so it would
become very stretched. But since the apatite and collagen in bone cohere
very tightly, then if the collagen is stretched to any extent the apatite will
be stretched far beyond its breaking strain and will become hopelessly

cracked. The collagen cannot 'reinforce' the apatite, like the steel in re-inforced concrete, any more than could rubber rods reinforce a bar of toffee.

The marrying of the properties of two different materials to produce a new *composite material* with very different properties is one of the triumphs of recent technology. It looks as though bone functions as a composite material. We can now review the different skeletal materials discussed in the last chapter from a new point of view. It seems, in fact, that we have a unifying principle making sense of the varied types of skeleton we see in animals.

In the corals, although the organic part is minute, the mineral is divided up into little needles. In brachiopods there is either a layered structure of mineral and organic sheets, or small needles of calcite are bound up in protein sheaths.

In arthropods the protein, even when tanned, is pliant in tension com-pared with the very stiff chitin, though in compression the protein's cross-links will prevent its buckling, while the chitin will buckle easily. In general, then, the protein can be thought of as acting as a matrix for the chitin. There are usually many layers in the cuticle. In each of these layers the chitin fibres are all orientated in the same direction in the plane of the layer. This direction is slightly different from the characteristic direction of the fibres in the neighbouring layers. In this way there are always layers particularly well suited to cope with any stresses acting in the plane of the cuticle. In crustaceans and millipedes, which often deposit calcite in the cuticle for extra stiffening, the calcite occurs as thin plates between $\frac{1}{2}$ and 5 μm thick. The amount of protein is reduced as the amount of calcite in-creases. This seems at first sight a little strange, because if the protein is acting as a matrix for the chitin fibres, one would expect the chitin, not the protein, to be replaced by the calcite. However, as the function of the calcite is presumably to increase the compressive stiffness and strength of the cuticle, it is probably more efficent to replace the relatively pliant protein by the very stiff calcite so that while in uncalcified cuticle the protein acts as a matrix for the chitin, in calcified cuticle the chitin, and what protein remains, acts as a matrix for the calcite.

The stiffer bryozoan skeletons are also composite, with separate crystals of calcite or aragonite in a protein/chitin matrix. The mollusc shell also has both a calcium carbonate and a protein part, and most of the calcium car-bonate is wrapped up in sheets of protein. Some weaker types have very little organic material. In these it is not known how the mineral is held together, but it does consist of many fine needles, and these probably separate at the approach of a crack.

Finally, to return to the vertebrates, enamel has a reasonable E for its low organic content, and it does have a composite structure. The large amount of water in it results in its variable value of E. The water is pushed out under high pressure. As this happens the stiffness increases markedly.

This may well be a means of preventing chipping, with a cushion of water being pressed out leaving a material of higher stiffness when the tooth bites hard.

This survey of the stiff materials in the main metazoan groups shows that almost universally the stiff, brittle components are separated from each other by organic sheets or matrices. Occasionally the organic content is so low that it cannot function in this way. But even in these cases the mineral seems always to be divided up into little needles or plates. There is one exception—the echinoderms.

With its extremely low organic content, and with its large elements made of single crystals, the echinoderm skeleton is a splendid example of the exception proving the rule. For, with their stereom structure, full of interconnecting cavities, the echinoderms seem to have found another way of stopping cracks. Any crack running through part of the stereom will always run quickly out into the large spaces, the stress concentration associated with the crack front will be lost, and the crack will not be propagated further. Also, the surface of the stereom is kept very smooth by the action of the cells permeating it (Plate 7); it is flaws on surfaces that are dangerous and most likely to cause crack-starting stress concentrations.

3.2   Orientated fibrous materials

Having dealt with the hard tissues we can look at the fibrous ones. They are of two kinds, materials in which all the fibres tend to be orientated in the same direction, and the rubbers, in which the fibres are arranged in a random network. They behave in rather different ways, and I shall deal with the orientated fibrous materials first.

Their main characteristic is that they are strong in tension but cannot resist much compression. They are strong in tension because they are not subjected to stress concentrations. If one fibril in a fibre made of thousands of fibrils breaks, the resulting increase in stress in each of the other fibrils is very small. A load has to break each fibril in turn, or make it slip past its neighbours, and there is no crack with high stress at the tip to aid the process. This is why tanning, or some analogous process producing lateral bonding between the chains, is necessary. The number of lateral links is important: too few and the fibrils will slip past each other, too many and the material will become too coherent and liable to stress concentrations.

The stiffness in tension of orientated fibrous materials can be quite high. Usually the stress-strain curve is concave upwards, with the stiffness increasing as the load increases. This is because initially the fibrils in the fibres tend to be wavy, and to have regions in which there is little preferred orientation. Little force is needed to straighten up the fibrils, but when they become aligned then the bonds with fixed valencies have to be distorted, and this requires much more force. The stiffness of fibres in compression is low for two reasons. One is that there are many bonds that are free to move in some directions, and the fibrils kink around these; in the same way a steel chain is effectively completely rigid in tension, but because the links are free cannot support any load in compression. The other is that the fibres are like a number of very slender columns, and we have seen that these are liable to collapse even if the material in them is quite stiff. Table 1 shows that collagen and keratin are much less stiff in tension than silk or cellulose or chitin. This is probably caused by the greater disorientation of the former fibres.

The properties of fibres can be very dependent on whether they are swollen with water or not. If water gets between the chains it hinders them from binding to each other, and so the chains can slip past each other, though this is hindered by entanglements. Many of the properties of materials with a fair amount of water are said to be *time dependent*. This means that the strain caused by a particular load does not all appear at once, but takes time.

One material with a great deal of water is cartilage. It consists of a polysaccharide-protein complex, large amounts of collagen and much water; as a result its mechanical properties are not easily understood. Despite its collagen it is not very strong in tension, probably because many of the fibres are not orientated along any particular direction of loading. It is somewhat stronger in compression, and has a rather low E. The mucopolysaccharide-protein complex is very attractive to water, so that when it is squeezed the water cannot easily be pushed out. The collagen probably functions to keep the whole mass coherent, and it also raises the E of the whole tissue by being fairly inextensible. In some cartilages the collagen forms a bag round the outside of the element, and so limits its change in shape. Cartilage is also important in joints, and will be discussed in this role in the next chapter.

Finally, although the function of orientated skeletal fibres is often to be strong in tension, as in spiders' silk and tendon, these fibres often have merely a space-filling or protective function, like much hair and the collagen and keratin of the skin.

3.3 Rubbers

Some skeletal materials are technically *rubbers*. They are made of long-chain proteins, with the chains running in all directions, joined here and there to each other. The three rubbers known in animals are resilin, elastin and abductin, though doubtless there are others. Resilin is found in many joints in arthropods, particularly in wing hinges. Elastin is found in vertebrates, for instance in artery walls and the vocal cords, and is particularly obvious in the ligamentum nuchae, the ligament running along the back of the neck in big grazing animals. Abductin is found in the hinge ligament of some bivalve molluscs that swim by clapping the valves of their shell rapidly.

These materials have in common a low stiffness, the ability to undergo very large strains, and a near perfect elasticity. This means that if you stretch or compress them and then let them do work as they recover you get almost as much work out of them as you put in. In resilin this return is about 94 per cent, compared with about 90 per cent for most commercial rubbers. This property makes them useful as energy stores. One use of resilin, in the flea, has been described. It is used in insect wing hinges so that muscles do not have actively to decelerate the wing at the end of each stroke. This braking is done by a pad of resilin, which uses the strain energy gained in the deceleration to accelerate the wing at the beginning of the next stroke. The almost perfect elasticity of resilin is important not only because it repays almost all the energy stored in it, but also because the energy is not degraded into heat. Waggle a thin sheet of steel back and forth quickly until it breaks, you will find it has become very hot. In the wing of an insect beating say five hundred times a second degradation of work into heat on this scale would have spectacular results. The elastin in arteries allows the arteries to expand as the heart contracts and then give back the energy more slowly, thus evening out pressure changes in the blood. The ligamentum nuchae enables large grazing animals to raise and lower their heads while grazing without making their muscles do all the work.

The rubbery properties of these materials are inherent, of course, in their structure. In resilin, for instance, there are about 60 amino acid residues in the chain, that are free, between each pair of junctions. The amino acids in the chain are such that there are many bonds with at least one axis about which they can rotate freely. As a result the chains are continually kinking, coiling and straightening under the influence of thermal agitation. One might think that, as the links are free to rotate, one could distort the mesh in any way one wished without having to perform any noticeable work. But this is not so. Although any orientation of the chain is theoretically possible, there is a *most likely* distance between the two ends of each bit of chain, and other lengths become increasingly unlikely to occur the further they are away from this most likely length. The most likely length is an intermediate one, with some of the bonds kinked, and some of them straight. It would be extremely improbable that the chain would be agitated into a completely straight configuration, or rolled up into a tight little ball. A rubber is made up of millions of these little chains, and all their lengthenings and shortenings are evened out, so that the block of rubber is effectively of constant size. If you compress rubber you are making the chains on average adopt a different, shorter configuration than they would otherwise. You are making them less probable, or decreasing their entropy, and the rubber will be in a state of stress. The thermal agitation will be tending to straighten the chains and you have to exert a force to keep the block compressed.

It should be clear from this discussion why rubbers are much less stiff than orientated fibres, and also why they can undergo such large elastic strains.

Joints 4

4.1 Types of joints

The function of joints is to provide a turning place between the stiff elements. Basically there are two kinds: those in which parts of the two elements *slide* on each other, so that problems of lubrication and wear arise, and those in which there is no sliding. Instead there is merely elastic *deformation* of some tissue. In this type of joint there is no problem about wear, though unless the tissue is perfectly elastic (which no tissue is) some energy will be lost in deforming it.

In joints, great freedom of action, and the ability to transfer large loads, tend to be incompatible. Joints like the knee, that move in only one plane, about one axis, can bear heavy loads without the necessity of a large number of muscles spanning the joint to keep it stable. A joint like the shoulder is incapable of taking really large loads, but is much freer. The jaws of the badger and of man make a similar pair. The badger's lower jaw is connected to the skull by two barrel joints that are such a good fit that the jaw often cannot be disarticulated even in the dried skull. The only motions the jaw muscles can bring about are opening and closing and a very slight movement in the direction of the line joining the two joints. The action of the jaw muscles is simple. The jaw of man can be moved, without changing its orientation: up and down, back and forth, and side to side. It can also be *rotated* about the anterior-posterior, vertical, and side-to-side axes. Therefore to describe the motion of the lower jaw relative to the skull requires the description of six independent motions, that may all be occurring simultaneously. Of course, particular motions may be rather restricted; we cannot rotate our jaws very much about the anterior-posterior axis, but it can be done. To produce this freedom the lower jaw has to be slung in a bag of muscle that must undergo very complex activity in order that the jaw may work efficiently.

4.2 Invertebrate joints

The arthropods and the vertebrates are the groups with well-developed joints, and the arthropods tend to be equipped with deformation joints more often than the vertebrates. This is because they have an exoskeleton. Joints can readily be made in exoskeletons by having rings of cuticle that are untanned and thinner than the cuticle of the adjoining elements. It is possible to have the ring folded in, as in Fig. 2–4, except at one place, which will then act as a hinge while the rest of the ring concertinas as required. The thin, untanned cuticle found in arthropod joints is called the arthrodial membrane (Fig. 2–4). A different system is seen where the wings of insects insert into the side wall of the thorax. Very frequently the wall at this place is made of a small block of resilin. This of course deforms easily, and is very efficient at storing energy.

Although the exoskeleton of arthropods is very suited for free joints, most joints that have to transmit forces cannot afford such freedom. In the arthropods many joints have one or two peg and socket joints between the two elements as well (Fig. 4–1). One peg and socket allows rotation about any axis passing through the joint, although the ability to rotate about the long axis of the element may be very restricted. Most arthropod joints have two such articulations, and these allow rotation only about the line joining them. A common trick of the arthropods is to have two joints close together along a limb, allowing rotation about different axes in successive joints. The consequence of this is that the elements separated by two joints can rotate reasonably freely relative to each other, yet each joint is strong.

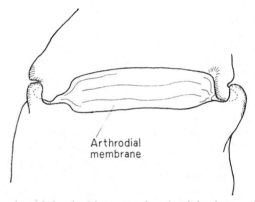

Fig. 4–1 Drawing of the double peg and socket joint in a crab's leg.

The peg and socket joint, though a very close fit, and allowing no play in unintended directions, is freely movable in permitted directions. It may or may not be covered by the arthrodial membrane that encloses the space between the two elements. It is very surprising to see, in the crab, for instance, very smooth bearing surfaces completely unprotected and exposed to the sea and sand. Nothing seems to be known about the lubrication of the pegs and sockets. Crabs, whose cuticle is rather hard because of the deposition of calcium carbonate, have a much softer cuticle covering the bearing surfaces of the pegs and sockets. This is a subject that would repay further study.

The bivalve molluscs have a simple fibrous protein hinge between the two valves, and the hard skeleton may articulate in a long cylindrical joint. In echinoderms the spines of echinoids (the sea urchins) have a small rounded cavity at their end which articulates with a boss on the surface of the test (the 'shell') of the animal. Round the base of the spine there are two fibrous cones attaching the spine to the body: an outer cone of muscle and an inner one made mainly of collagen. Presumably the collagen keeps the spine tight on the boss, and the muscle is concerned with the orientation of the spine. But this is somewhat peculiar, because the collagen should relax slightly under load, in which case nearly all the clamping would have to be done by the muscle. There do seem to be some contractile fibres among the collagen, but not many, and their function is unknown. The characteristic echinoderm stereom structure is found at the bearing surfaces, which are therefore covered with small holes. They also, however, have long gutters that may contain some kind of lubricating fluid. Even so, the speed and frequency of rotation of the spines is small and lubrication, or the lack of it, cannot be very important. It has, however, been observed in some animals that the tubercule is abraded by the action of the base of the spine.

4·3   Vertebrate joints

The main skeletal elements of vertebrates are bones of course. The usual kind of movable joint between these is called a synovial joint (Fig. 1–5). The ends of the two bones are expanded and covered with a layer of cartilage. The bearing surfaces are in a cavity, the synovial cavity, which contains synovial fluid. This fluid has a composition similar to that of blood plasma, but with less protein and with the addition of a mucopolysaccharide, hyaluronic acid, some of which is bound to protein. Not shown in Fig. 1–5 are the various ligaments connecting the ends of the two bones, allowing them to move relative to each other in certain directions only. Synovial joints are remarkable for their very low coefficient of friction, which can be as little as 0·005, lower than many engineering bearings.

When two surfaces slide on one another friction is caused because the two surfaces are, at the microscopic level, very rough. They therefore tend to touch at only a few high points, and the total area in contact is much less than would seem. This means that the force acting across the surfaces is carried at few points, and so stresses are locally very high. The material of the surfaces may become crushed and, in the case of metals, welded or joined in some other way. These junctions have to be sheared off as the two surfaces slide past one another.

Lubrication is of two main types. In boundary lubrication the two surfaces are separated by a layer of lubricant only a few molecules thick, and in places the two surfaces may still touch. The lubricant may be adsorbed to the surfaces. The lubricant molecules partially fill up the cavities between the surfaces, so that the pressure is more evenly spread. Furthermore, the lubricant molecules tend to stick to each other less than do the molecules of the joint surfaces, and this inhibits the formation of junctions. Boundary lubrication can produce quite low coefficients of friction, but much lower ones can be produced by 'fluid film' lubrication. In this there is an appreciable thickness of lubricating fluid between the two surfaces, and resistance to sliding is now produced only by the work necessary to shear the fluid. This is of course much less than the work necessary to shear off solid asperities, and produces negligible wear.

The difficult thing about fluid film lubrication is to keep the thin film of liquid intact when there is considerable pressure between the two surfaces tending to squeeze it out. In engineering practice lubricant may be forcibly pumped into the gap, or the shapes of the bearing surfaces may be arranged so that as they move relative to each other the lubricant has no option but to squeeze through the gap between the surfaces. This causes a high pressure locally in the lubricant, and this keeps the two surfaces apart. This is called 'hydrodynamic' lubrication. In 'squeeze film' lubrication use is simply made of the ability of many lubricants to cohere as continuous films, even under high pressure, and so to resist being squeezed out from between the bearing surfaces.

The coefficient of friction of synovial joints is so low that it is almost certain that some kind of fluid film lubrication is acting so the problem is, how is the fluid film maintained under pressure? There are various suggestions, and the whole subject is in a state of flux, but what follows is roughly what many people think might be happening. When a joint is moving rapidly with little load on it then there is hydrodynamic lubrication. This is helped by the low stiffness of the cartilage, which allows potential asperities to deform and flatten as the pressure in the synovial fluid increases locally. If the load across the joint is large, however, the nature of the surfaces becomes important. The cartilage surface is very rough by engineering standards, having undulations about 2–4 μm high and 30–50 μm from crest to crest all over the surface. When the two surfaces approach under load the high points will come very close, leaving innumerable cavities in which the synovial fluid will be trapped (Fig. 4–2.) The water within the high parts of the cartilage will be under great pressure and will migrate into the pockets of trapped synovial fluid which will be at a lower pressure. This will in turn increase the pressure in the pockets. so that the synovial fluid will be bearing a large part of the total load. As the pressure increases water will tend to migrate back into the cartilage, but the molecules of the hyaluronic acid/protein complex are too long for it to do this, so the synovial fluid will become more and more concentrated, and will be very resistant to being squeezed out sideways from between the bearing surfaces. Even the high points will not be rubbing against each other because as the pressure increases the hyaluronic acid forms coherent sheets that remain between the cartilage surfaces.

In short it seems that hydrodynamic, boundary and squeeze film lubrication are all used to some extent, and there is the added refinement of the trapped pockets of synovial fluid changing their properties as the pressure increases.

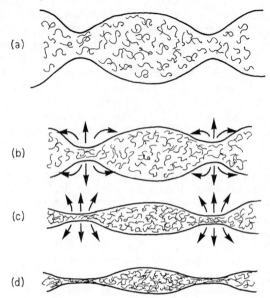

Fig. 4–2   Diagram of the sequence of events as the two joint surfaces in a synovial joint are pressed closer together. The long-chain molecules of the hyaluronic acid/protein complex are indicated by squiggles. (a) The surfaces approach. (b) As the peaks come together water is forced into the cartilage at the high points. Some escapes into the synovial cavity elsewhere. The direction of water movement is indicated by arrows. (c) As the process continues the long chain molecules become more concentrated. (d) The cartilage is much flattened, there are trapped pools of concentrated synovial fluid.

Where only limited movement between bones is required the vertebrates employ a system rather like the arthropods—a less stiff part is inserted between two stiff elements. This is seen, for example, between many mammalian vertebrae, where the cartilage cap of each vertebra is joined to the next by very collagenous fibrous cartilage.

The Hydrostatic Skeleton

In the hydrostatic skeleton, employed by many animals, use is made of the fact that water, although not at all viscous, is virtually incompressible. Therefore, any closed container with flexible walls, filled with water, may be able to change its shape, but it cannot change its volume.

5.1 Lophophorates

A fairly simple example of the use of the hydrostatic skeleton can be seen in lophophorate animals. These are filter feeders who extend a funnel of hollow finger-like tentacles, known as the lophophore, into the water. Particles suspended in the water stick to these fingers and are carried by cilia to the mouth. Lophophorates occur in many different groups. They are sessile and live in tubes or skeletal boxes for protection.

The lophophore is extended by the contraction of the muscles of the body wall. This raises the internal pressure and the lophophore is extended and kept stiff like the fingers of a rubber glove when you blow into it. If one of the tentacles were to collapse the water from it would correspondingly increase the volume of the main body of the animal. Such collapse is therefore resisted by the hydrostatic pressure. If the animal is threatened in any way the lophophore is withdrawn into the tube or shell. This is done by retractor muscles, which attach to the base of the lophophore. Of course, as the lophophore is withdrawn into the body of the animal the body wall muscles must relax to allow the body to expand, as the total volume of the animal must remain the same. In mud this is no difficulty, but if the animal is protected by a *rigid* skeleton there is a problem, because the lophophore is being forced into something that is already full. The bryozoa face this problem. They are colonial animals, encrusting seaweed and rock and, in those that we are interested in, each individual lives in a small calcareous box. In one group the outer face does not have skeletal protection, so that the covering membrane can bulge out when the lophophore is withdrawn (Fig. 5–1(a)–(d)). Conversely, when the lophophore is to be extended muscles, attached to the outer membrane, contract and the resulting increase in hydrostatic pressure pushes the lophophore out. It is, of course, better to present a flat membrane to a predator than a number of delicate fingers but even so the arrangement could be improved, as is shown by a second group. In these the body of the animal has a calcareous skeleton on its outer face, but it has holes in it, and outside it is a membrane that functions like the outer membrane of the first group (Fig. 5–1(e)–(h)). A third group has evolved a structure called a compensation sac (Fig. 5–1 (i)–(l)). When the lophophore is extended the compensation sac is full of water. When the retractor muscles withdraw the lophophore the sac is emptied. When the lophophore is to be extended muscles attached to the compensation sac pull it open, water from the outside rushes in to fill it and the lophophore is forced out. Because of this cunning device the animal, when withdrawn, is completely covered by skeletal walls except for the small opening for the lophophore and the compensation sac mouth.

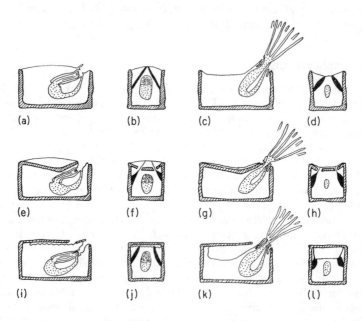

Fig. 5–1 Some bryozoan hydrostatic skeletons. Each row shows a different mechanism. The two left hand diagrams are side and end views of the retracted state, the two right hand ones are of the extended state. Hard skeleton cross-hatched, body stippled, muscles solid black.

5.2 Earthworms

The lophophorates use the hydrostatic skeleton to change their shape, but not to exert any real force on the environment. Most worms, however, use a hydrostatic skeleton for locomotion. A familiar example is the earthworm. Its body-wall muscles are of two types, longitudinal and circular. Suppose, in a burrow, the worm needs to push its front end into the earth. It can do this by anchoring the back end of the body to the sides of the burrow with bristles or chaetae while at the front end the circular muscles contract and the longitudinal ones relax. This will tend to make the front end long and thin, and so push it into the earth. But calculations show that the longitudinal muscles by their contraction are able to cause a much higher hydrostatic pressure (when the worm is getting fatter) than the circular muscles (when the worm is getting longer). Probably the worm uses its front end as a seeker rather than a battering ram and the burrow is made by the body, which has been inserted into a narrow crevice, expanding.

The body is divided into compartments by cross-walls, the septa. There are muscles in the septal walls whose function is to prevent the wall from bulging very much if there is a pressure difference between adjoining segments. The result of this is that pressure changes are restricted to short lengths of the body, so that if longitudinal muscles are exerting a great

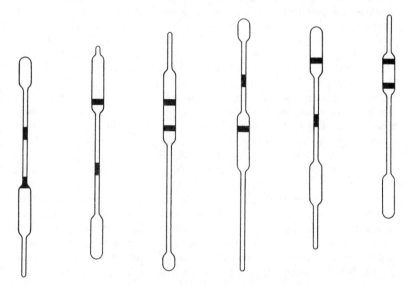

Fig. 5-2 Diagrams of an earthworm crawling. In the fat regions the chaetae are extended, anchoring the body to the walls of the burrow. Two segments are shown black so one can see how they change their shape and their distance from one another. Note that the waves pass backward down the body as the worm moves forward.

force in one part of the body there is no necessity for the circular muscles along the whole length of the body to be active in order to prevent the whole worm from thickening and shortening. That this is an important consideration can be seen from Fig. 5-2 where the motions of an earthworm burrowing are shown. There are waves of extension and shortening passing down the body, and most of the time there are two thin regions. If all the pressure changes were transmitted right along the body the muscles would all be working against each other, and much of their effort would be irrelevant to what was going on in their own part of the body.

5.3   Nematodes

The hydrostatic skeleton of nematodes is peculiar. They do not have the circular muscles found in other worms, only longitudinal ones. Now muscles can exert a force only when they contract, they cannot actively extend themselves. One of the functions of the hydrostatic skeleton is to force contracted muscles to extend, so that they can contract and do work again. In most worms the circular and longitudinal muscles antagonise each other and as one set contracts the other is forced to extend. Nematodes have a thick cuticle capable of withstanding high internal pressure. The pressure in nematodes can be 53 000 N m^{-2} of mercury when the animal is active, compared with 600 to at most 10 000 N m^{-2} in other animals with hydrostatic skeletons. The tension-resisting collagen fibres of the cuticle of nematodes wind round the worm in a helix, and at any point make an angle of about 75° with the longitudinal axis of the worm. What would be the effect of changing this angle? Clearly, if the helix was stretched out so that the angle approached 0° the worm would be very long and the volume would be near zero also. Similarly, if the angle approached 90° this would imply a very fat worm of effectively no length, so that the volume would again approach zero. In fact the maximum volume would be at a fibre angle of about 55°. An *increase* of volume, of course, implies a *reduction* of hydrostatic pressure. Since the worm has a high internal pressure it will always tend to increase in length, so that the fibre angle will be nearer 55°. Of course, there could not be any actual change in volume if this angle were achieved, but the fibres would become slacker, and the cross-section of the worm would become elliptical instead of circular producing a smaller cross-sectional area although the circumference remains nearly constant. The increase in length is resisted by the longitudinal muscles. So, if the longitudinal muscles relax the internal pressure will increase the length of the worm. In life it seems that the muscles rarely relax far. If the muscles attempt to contract the volume cannot change, of course, so the internal pressure increases. The upshot of all this is that the muscles can contract on one side of the animal, and when they relax they are extended again by the hydrostatic pressure. In this way the nematode can be thrown into curves and so can progress.

5.4   Burrowing

We have seen how the earthworm burrows, but many animals use a specialised proboscis of some kind. This need not necessarily be part of the front end of the body, in fact in many molluscs the foot may act as a kind of proboscis. The essence of the function of a proboscis is that it is extended with some force as a narrow cylinder through the substrate, and then swells. The swelling anchors it and then the rest of the body is pulled up to the proboscis. The system is well shown in *Priapulus*. (Priapulids are a group of unsegmented worms of uncertain relationships.) The animal has a proboscis that can be withdrawn inside the body (Fig. 5–3(a)). The circular and longitudinal muscles of the body contract simultaneously shooting the proboscis out forcibly so that it squirts through the mud (Fig. 5–3(b)). Further contraction of the circular body muscles forces more fluid into the proboscis and it expands, particularly at the tip. At the same time a small part of the back end of the animal remains expanded so that the animal does not move backwards (Fig. 5–3(c)). The longitudinal muscles contract (Fig. 5–3(d)) moving the body over the proboscis until it disappears inside (Fig. 5–3(e)).

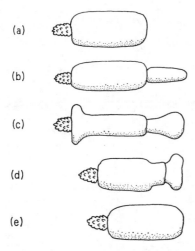

Fig. 5–3   The burrowing of *Priapulus*.

5.5 Echinoderms

One group of animals, the echinoderms, uses the hydrostatic skeleton in quite a different way. Echinoderms have, with few exceptions, an external covering of skeletal plates that makes them rather inflexible. They have developed a remarkable *water-vascular* system consisting of a series of tubes called radial canals running from a tubular ring round the mouth. The system contains a coelomic fluid not very different from sea water, though it does contain floating cells. The radial canals give off finger-like processes called podia or tube feet. Their structure varies, but we can take the tube foot of a regular echinoid (a sea urchin) as a well developed example (Fig. 5–4). It is long and cylindrical, with retractor muscles along its length and with circular collagen fibres. The end is expanded into a disc stiffened internally by a ring of calcareous ossicles called a rosette. Above the rosette there is a little stack of ossicles which acts as a support for muscles that pull up the middle of the disc when it is attached to the ground, so forming a partial vacuum. Copious mucus secretion from cells in the disc helps it to stick. In locomotion the tube feet are extended and pointed in any direction as necessary by means of the differential contraction of the longitudinal muscles on different sides. They then stick to the substrate and are shortened by the longitudinal muscles. In this way the urchin is pulled over the substrate. Extension of the tube foot is made possible by its ampulla, which lies inside the test of the urchin and has muscle fibres all round it. There is a valve between the tube-foot/ampulla system and the radial canal, so that

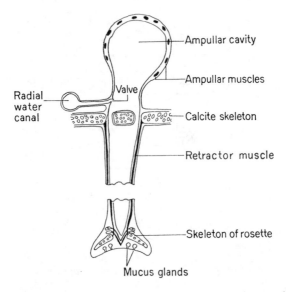

Fig. 5–4 Diagram of the tube foot of an echinoid. Muscles are shown solid black. The gap indicates that the length to thickness ratio can be very great.

the tube foot can extend and retract without involving the rest of the system. Although each tube foot is small compared with the size of the urchin there are several thousand of them, so that if they were all to retract at the same time, as might happen in an emergency, there would be a marked increase in the volume of water inside the test. There is a connection between the water-vascular system and the outside world, called the madreporite, but it does not seem to act as a safety valve in these circumstances. Instead there is a flexible membrane round the mouth and this bulges outwards as the tube feet retract. However, usually the urchin arranges things so that as many feet are extended as are retracted.

This is the 'standard' echinoid tube foot. The range of functions of tube

feet over all the echinoderms is very great. They can be suckered, as described, or they can be pointed and tough at the end for burrowing through
the sand. In one group, the crinoids, they are used for feeding, forcing food
particles into a mucus trap by violent flinging movements. Some tube feet
are sensory. In some burrowers there are calcareous scrapers embedded in
the tube feet used to keep respiratory tunnels to the sufrace clear. Some
tube feet are just respiratory, serving as a convenient way of bringing
coelomic fluid very close to the sea water. All this great variety of form and
function depends on the ability of some part of the system to keep up the
hydrostatic pressure that forces the tube feet to extend.

5.6 Spiders' legs

Spiders, and some other arachnids, have developed a peculiar system for
moving their legs. They have no extensor muscles and so cannot straighten
their legs by muscular action. Instead they pump their legs straight. By
the action of muscles in the body of the spider the hydrostatic pressure in
the legs is increased, and this makes the joints straighten out rather like the
party toy you blow down which then uncurls and makes a horrid braying
noise. It is interesting that, of the many arthropod legs I have looked at,
it is only some jumping spiders that have extremely thin walled legs in
relation to their overall diameter. We saw on page 7 that this is a dangerous condition because the walls are likely to buckle. But in jumping spiders
the greatest stresses in the legs are likely to occur at the moment of jumping.
It is just at this time that the legs are stiffened by the increased internal
pressure, and so buckling is avoided.

Further Reading

ALEXANDER, R. MCN. (1968). *Animal mechanics.* Sidgwick & Jackson, London (deals more rigorously than this book with some of the problems discussed in Chapter 1)

BENNET-CLARK, H. C. and LUCEY, E. C. A. (1967). The jump of the flea. *J. exp. Biol.* **47**, 59–76 (a clear account of this amusing problem)

CLARK, R. B. (1964). *Dynamics in metazoan evolution.* University Press, Oxford (good account of the hydrostatic skeleton)

CONNELL, J. H. (1961). Effects of competition, predation by *Thais lapillus* and other factors on natural populations of the barnacle *Balanus balanoides. Ecol. monogr.* **31**, 61–104 (whelks with thick and thin shells)

CURREY, J. D. (1967). The failure of exoskeletons and endoskeletons. *J. morph.* **123**, 1–16 (a deeper treatment of the differences between endo- and exoskeletons)

CURREY, J. D. (1970). The mechanical properties of bone. *Clin. Orthop.* **73,** 210–231. (A recent survey)

CURREY, J. D. and TAYLOR, J. D. (1974). The mechanical behaviour of some molluscan hard tissues. *J. Zool. Lond.,* **173**, 395–406.

FLORKIN, M. and STOTZ, E. H. (1968). *Comprehensive Biochemistry.* Vol 26. Elsevier, London (Three volumes giving a good account of many of the matters dealt with in Chapter 2)

FRANKEL, V. H. and BURSTEIN, A. H. (1970). *Orthopaedic Biomechanics: The application of engineering to the musculoskeletal system.* Lea and Febinger, Philadelphia (a very clear book)

GORDON, J. E. (1968). *The new science of strong materials.* Pelican, London (a clear and humorous introduction to a difficult subject)

JENSEN, M. and WEIS-FOGH, T. (1962). Strength and elasticity of locust cuticle. *Phil. Trans. Roy. Soc. B.* **245**, 137–69 (the first major attack on the mechanics of an invertebrate skeletal material)

RAUP, D. M. (1966). Geometric analysis of shell coiling: general problems. *J. Palaeont.* **40**, 1178–90 (the mathematical treatment of shell form. Will probably become a classic)

TAYLOR, J. D., KENNEDY, W. J. and HALL, A. (1969). The shell structure and mineralogy of the bivalvia. Introduction. Nuculacea-Trigonacea. *Bull. Brit. Mus. (Nat. Hist.) Zool.* Suppl. 3; (1973), Lucinacea-Clavagellacea. *Bull. Brit. Mus. (Nat. Hist.) Zool.,* **22**, No. 9 (Accounts, with many illustrations, of bivalve shell types)

THOMPSON, D'ARCY, W. (1942). *On growth and form.* Cambridge University Press, London (a classic of scientific writing)

WAINWRIGHT, S. A. and DILLON, J. R. (1969). On the orientation of sea fans (genus *Gorgonia). Biol. Bull.* **136**, 130–139 (the differences in the mechanics of hard and soft corals)